Let's Spe

Stories from t̶.̶ ̶.̶.̶.̶.̶.̶ ̶Diaspora on
Cuisine, Community, and Culture

EDITED BY Cindy Similien-Johnson

CSJ Media Publishing • New York

Let's Speak Haitian Food: stories from the haitian diaspora on cuisine, community, and culture/ edited by Cindy Similien-Johnson
p. cm.

1.Haitian Cuisine 2. Caribbean Cuisine 3. Food 4. Community
5. Culture 6. Food 7. Title

Book Published and Designed by:
CSJ Media Publishing
Email: csjmediapublishing@gmail.com
Website: www.csjmediapublishing.com

In loving memory of
Philomène Elie Beaubrun,
my grandmother.

Acknowledgments

I would like to thank:

God, through my Lord and Savior Jesus Christ, for His love. For with You, all things are possible!

My family and friends - I am, because we are.

Grandma Philomène, for your legacy of love in action; and, Grandpa Oreste, for your legacy of community activism.

Rev. Dr. Herbert Daughtry and his family, for instilling the politics, pride, and purpose in me over the years. I am forever grateful. Thank you for teaching me the importance of knowing my history and writing my own story.

My Haitian brothers and sisters, for sharing your stories. Thank you, Abigail Lowe, Aganthina Nozy, Alexandra Josephine Morquette, Alexandra Spesest, Alix Chery, Andrea Graham, Berlotte Antoine, Carmel Balan, Cathy Delaleu, Charlotte Clark, Ciano Clerjuste, Claudine Mondesir, Daniella Bien-Aime, Daphne Ferdinand, Daphnie Bordes, Debbie Jean-Jacques, Denice Chinn, Dina Simon, Dr. Evelyn Julmisse, Dr. Jean Alerte, Dr. Jeff Gardere, Dr. Mireille Lauture, Ed Gehy, Edwidge Danticat, Elsie Augustave, Elsie Chery, Errold Moy Michel, Esther Simon, Fabienne Sylvia Josaphat-Merritt, Fabiola Jean, Farrah M. J. Louis, Fedia Louis, Florcy Morisset, Franchesca Fontus, Garland Viaud, Guerda Noel, Huguens

Mercier, Ingrid Austin Daniels, Jasmine Belotte, Jasmyn Crawford, Jean Aluc, Jean Appolon, Jean Eddy Saint Paul, Ph.D., Jessica Descartes, Joseph Makhandal Champagne, Josue Pierre, Kat Cherie, Katia D. Ulysse, Keylah Mellon, Kristia Beaubrun, Liliane Nerette-Louis, Lorraine Charles, Lucie Monestime, Lulu Orange Tyson, Lynnsie Augustin, Mandaly C. Louis-Charles, Margarette Tropnas, Marjorie Vail, Mary Leon Bourjolly, Mathylde Frontus, Maureen Boyer, Medjy Mezilus, Melissa P. Bernier, Mohan Jean-Mary, Myriam Jean, Myriam-Skye Holly, Myrlande Georges, Nadege Fleurimond, Nadine St. Julien, Naomie Dieduonne, Nedgine Paul Deroly, Nyska Merisier-Desarmes, Olivier Duong, Patricia Brintle, Paul Celicourt, Paulette Salisbury, Philomène Beaubrun, Rachel Charles, Rebecca Alfred, Richard Louissant, Rodney Pepe-Souvenir, Romel Edmond, Sabene Similien, Serge Renaud, Soraya Denis Volcy, Stacey Toussaint, Stephanie Scherpf, Stephanie Senat, Steve Similien, Susie Pepe, Suze Guillaume, Tahira Pierre-Cadet, Tamarre Torchon, Tracey F. Laroche, Tracy Guiteau, Vanessa Leon, Vania André, Vicki Sylvain, Vie Ciné, Vladimir Lévêque, Wanda Tima-Gilles, Wynnie Lamour, Yamilee Toussaint, Yanick J.P. Lahens, Yvana Romelus, and Yve-Car Momperousse.

I am not Haitian because I was born in Haiti,
I am Haitian because Haiti was born in me.
-Anonymous

Every generation needs a cultural revolution.
-Rev. Dr. Herbert Daughtry

Table of Contents

Introduction

Author Cindy Similien-Johnson
with her grandmother, Philomène Elie Beaubrun,
November 3, 2012

On November 3, 2012, I met my grandmother, Philomène Elie Beaubrun, for the first time in 20 years. She came to visit us in New York City from Haiti after making a stop in Florida to visit other family members.

As I greeted her, the first thing she asked me was, "Eske ou sonje mwen, pitit mwen?" in her sing-song Creole. "Do you remember me?"

"Wi, mwen sonje ou," I replied in my inexpert Creole as she embraced me. Of course, I remembered her. How could I forget? Oftentimes, I would reminisce about the time I visited her in Haiti when I was a young girl. Her backyard was filled with coconut, mango, and banana trees. She had a small farm with chickens, pigs, and goats. I remember eating her rich, savory meals like *Mayi Moulen* (Cornmeal Porridge) served with *Sòs Pwa Nwa* (Black Bean Sauce), and *Diri Blan* (White Rice) with *Poul nan Sòs* (Chicken in Sauce). Those early childhood memories stayed with me throughout the years. Even though I was born and raised in the U.S.A., I still felt a connection to Haiti as though there was an invisible umbilical cord attached between my heart and the country.

After being away from Haiti for many years, I was in awe to be in the presence of my grandmother – my *Haitian* grandmother, a centenarian. (At the time, she was 102 years old.) She was, as the French say, "eternellement jeune" (eternally young). She contained an unspeakable love and joy in the bosom of her heart that permeated her whole being as she spoke of moments long gone and sang hymns. She embodied unsurpassed strength and wisdom.

My grandmother expressed gratitude to God for the breath in her lungs and the opportunity to see her "*pitit and pitit pitit*" – her children, grandchildren, and even her great-

13

grandchildren. She imparted timeless wisdom about life, and shared stories about members of the family.

I was told that she narrowly survived the devastating earthquake that struck Haiti on January 12, 2010. After the earthquake, Haiti was no longer a distant childhood memory. People from around the world were now talking about the country, and it was on the news every day. Google even added a "Haitian Creole" language translation feature whereas only a few weeks before I had remarked the lack of inclusivity. I participated in a Prayer Service held at The House of the Lord Church in Brooklyn, NY where Rev. Dr. Herbert Daughtry, the renowned Civil Rights Activist, gathered local community leaders in solidarity and support of Haiti. I sang a poem I had penned the night I first received the news about the earthquake: *"Kenbe la, manman, papa, frè, sè."* (Hold on, my mother, father, brother, sister.)

Seven years later, in January 2017, I came across an online article that was originally published in the Toronto Star on January 26, 2010. My grandmother was mentioned in it. The journalist, after detailing the aftermaths of the earthquake and the plight of those who were displaced, wrote, "Philomene Elie is one of them. She turns 100 this July. She was sleeping in bed when the walls of her daughter's apartment cracked. Her grandson Ronald rushed in, scooped her up and carried her outside. They spent three days sleeping in a park besides mounting corpses, before a distant acquaintance found her scared and confused, and drove her here."

Yes, it was a great honor and privilege to be in the presence of my grandmother. When it was time for me to leave that evening, she held onto my hands to bless me as was the usual custom of the elders in a Haitian family. Her grip was so strong. Her hands fastened to mine. The skin on the back of her hands felt delicate like a rose petal and smooth like a polished stone.

As she blessed me, the idea for this book came to mind. I wanted to hold on to the precious memories of my Haitian upbringing. It was in that moment I realized the importance of passing down memories, traditions, and stories to the next generation.

Growing up, somehow (and unfortunately), I became disconnected from my roots. I lost my sense of cultural identity as I navigated through adolescence and early adulthood. For most of my life, I was standing on the fence, on the border, on the dash between Haitian and American. However, after meeting my grandmother, I was on a quest to learn everything I could about my Haitian heritage. There's an African proverb that says, "We must go back to our roots to move forward." I read books and articles about Haiti. With each new information that I received, I was empowered. In knowing who I am and where I came from, I developed a strong sense of cultural identity. By being more fully and truly myself, I was also able to relate to others on a better and deeper level without compromise.

I learned that Haiti was the first Black republic to gain its independence from colonial rule. That explained our resilience and perseverance. I traced my roots back to Jérémie, a province in Haiti known as "the city of poets" because many writers, poets, and historians were born there. That explained my desire to write a book of this nature - the love of storytelling runs in my blood! A couple of years ago, I learned that my grandfather was a business

15

owner and a former mayor in Moron, Haiti. That explained my social entrepreneurial pursuits.

I rediscovered the musical beats of Kompa and Zouk which played at the Baptism and Communion parties I had attended as a child. The men and women always had a particular style of dancing – their bodies swayed perfectly to the rhythm and beat of every song - *back and forth, back and foth.*

I frequented my old neighborhood known as "Little Haiti" in Brooklyn, NY due to the large Haitian population in an area bordered by Flatbush and Church Avenues. During my visits, I caught pieces of conversations from the passersby, hearing the familiar "Sak Pase? M'ap Boule" and "Bondye Bon." However, the women street vendors, who sold *Jirof* (Cloves), *Tablèt Pistache* (Peanut Brittle), *Pikliz* (Spicy Coleslaw) in glass jars, red and white jumbo mint balls, and other delicacies, along Church Avenue were no longer in sight. I always made a stop at the local Haitian bakery to order at least two *Patés Kodes* (Haitian patties) and a bottle of Cola Lacaye's champagne soda.

Whenever I attempted to speak Haitian Creole, it felt unfamiliar on my tongue as if my mouth was filled with gravel. As a child, I was defiant and refused to speak Haitian Creole because it didn't seem like the popular thing to do. When relatives spoke to me in Creole, I would always respond in English. I regret being so stubborn. I know it's never too late to learn Creole, but there's a void - I missed 20-plus years of molding and shaping the language into my own. It will take time, practice, and patience to master the art of the language.

However, it was through food that I felt a deeper connection to my Haitian roots. I grew up eating Haitian food. I had *Soup Joumou* (Pumpkin Soup) every Christmas, Thanksgiving, and especially on New Year's Day. At every Baptism, Communion, Wedding, and Graduation, dishes like *Banan Peze* (Fried Plantains), *Diri Djon-Djon* (Black Mushroom Rice), and *Griot* (Fried Pork) were always served. A Haitian party was not a party without Griot!

Food always brings back a flood of memories. A whiff of cinnamon or ginger always takes me back to the time when relatives from Haiti brought a hard, dense-like cake called *Konparèt* wrapped in foil paper in their black *malèt* or *valiz* (luggage). Any crispy, flaky pastry reminds me of the *Patés Kodes* which were served at Communion and Baptism parties.

Consequently, I began cooking and compiling the recipes of the meals I used to eat during my childhood. About a year ago, I wrote and published the "Cook Like A Haitian" cookbook series as a way to preserve traditional Haitian recipes, and help others of Haitian descent like myself reconnect to their heritage through food.

A famed artist once said, "I begin with an idea and then it becomes something else." I started this project as a cookbook, but what you hold in your hands is a culmination of half a decade worth of collecting, editing, and compiling stories from more than 100 members of the Haitian Diaspora. I knew I was not the only one who had childhood memories of food. I reached out to my Haitian brothers and sisters from around the world, and they voluntarily shared their heartfelt stories with me. Among the group are one or two "honorary Haitians" who have expressed great appreciation for Haitian cuisine.

You will oftentimes see yourself in the stories of my Haitian brothers and sisters. Some will make you laugh,

17

cry, or even cherish your own moments of "meals and memories." I am truly honored and eternally grateful for their contributions.

A fellow Haitian sister once said, "We are the keepers of our legacy." This project was a huge undertaking, but a worthy mission. It started as a simple thought on the night I first met my grandmother, and it evolved into something else. I have to admit that this project is not complete; there are more stories to tell. I wish I could include the thoughts of every person in the Haitian Diaspora in this book but that is not feasible. It would require more books than this earth could hold. However, it is my hope that this book cultivates the importance of sharing our stories, traditions, and memories; and, passing them on to the next generation. We must always remember and celebrate our Haitian cuisine, community, and culture.

At the end of this book, I include some of my favorite recipes from my childhood. (For more recipes, please visit cooklikeahaitian.wordpress.com. You can also download my bestselling "Cook Like A Haitian" cookbook series on Amazon.com.) Additionally, at the end of this book, I offer a glimpse of Haiti's music, culture, language, history, and literature. Thank you for reading, and may our stories continue to live on!

Nan tèt ansanm, in solidarity,

Cindy Similien-Johnson

Let's Speak Haitian Food

*Stories from the Haitian Diaspora on
Cuisine, Community, and Culture*

▲▲▲▲▲▲▲▲▲▲▲▲▲▲▲▲▲▲▲▲▲▲▲▲▲▲

My favorite Haitian meal is Diri Djon-Djon ak Tassot Turkey (Black Mushroom Rice with Fried Turkey). Some of my fond memories of eating Haitian food included family gatherings and holidays. My family and I are originally from New York, and although all of us have moved to different places over the years, I can't help but reflect on how significant of a role Haitian food had in our expressions to one another.

When my grandparents were still alive, all family functions were done at their home and a lot of my cherished memories took place between those walls. The richness and cultural aspects incorporated into Haitian food have definitely impacted the person I am today.

As a Haitian woman, it was expected for me to learn how to cook, specifically "Haitian Food." As my grandmother would say, "Fo'w kon fe manje Ayisyen! (You have to know how to cook Haitian food!)." I'm truly grateful for my experiences and look forward to sharing my love and respect for Haitian food with my family and generations to come.

Franchesca Fontus, Writer

▲▲▲▲▲▲▲▲▲▲▲▲▲▲▲▲▲▲▲▲▲▲▲▲▲▲▲

My favorite Haitian meal is baked fish and yams. I remember that whenever my mother and grandmother cooked, the smell always embodied the entire neighborhood.

Jean Appolon, Co-founder/Artistic Director of
Jean Appolon Expressions

▲▲▲▲▲▲▲▲▲▲▲▲▲▲▲▲▲▲▲▲▲▲▲▲▲▲▲▲▲

My dad owned a sugar cane plantation when I was very young so we drank the juice during meals. I wonder if maybe that is where I got my love for sweets. It seems that breakfast sticks in my mind more than any other meal.

Childhood memories come in dribs and drabs, sort of like flashes or snippets of a movie, but the one that lingers the most is having avocado and bread (like a squaring roll) with a cup of Akasan (Cornmeal Drink), or Haran Saur (Eggs with Herring) and a boiled unripe purple banana on the side for breakfast before heading out to school.

Patricia Brintle, Artist

▲ ▲

Legim (Legumes) tops everything. Not only is it delicious, it's hands down the most healthy. It includes all the vegetables that you normally wouldn't consume - carrots, spinach, kale, chayotes, tomatoes, cabbage - all in one dish. The thing about Legim is that it can be eaten by itself, or as a side dish.

Kat Cherie, Founder of Kreyolicious

▲ ▲

I have so many favorite Haitian foods, but my all-time favorites are Aransò ak Banan (Herring with Plantains). My grandma used to make it all the time, and I always think of her when I eat it now.

Wynnie Lamour, Founder & Managing Director of
Haitian Creole Language Institute of New York

▲▲▲▲▲▲▲▲▲▲▲▲▲▲▲▲▲▲▲▲▲▲▲▲▲

My favorite Haitian meal is Legim and spaghetti with Aransò (Herring). My most memorable time eating Haitian food was in Haiti last year. It was my first time visiting my father's home in Marchand, Dessalines. He lives in New York, but visits Haiti regularly. I was surprised to see the many people who lived in the housing complex. Six women and three men lived at the lower level.

The women would cook breakfast, lunch, and dinner every day. One day, they cooked the most delicious Legim and white rice I had ever tasted. It had crab legs, beef, and huge chunks of fresh vegetables. We finished everything by the end of the night. I couldn't stop raving how incredible the meal was and that I could eat it every day for the rest of our trip.

Someone must have told them what I had said because the very next day, during lunch, there was a fresh pot of Legim - more plentiful than the day before. We ate every last bit of that one as well.

Tahira Pierre-Cadet, Licensed Real Estate Salesperson

▲▲▲▲▲▲▲▲▲▲▲▲▲▲▲▲▲▲▲▲▲▲▲▲▲▲▲

Espageti Ak Aransò (Spaghetti with Herring) is my favorite Haitian dish. It's my little piece of home. Although other cultures have their own versions of this dish, no one does it quite like Haitians. Growing up, this dish was a staple in our house. We ate it for breakfast, lunch, or dinner. It's a dish that can be found in any Haitian household no matter what social class you belong to. I've even given the traditional recipe my own twist.

My most memorable time eating Haitian food was having dinner with my mother on Sundays. I was raised by a single mom. She owned a business and did not have time to cook during the week when I was growing up. She left the cooking to our cook.

But Sundays... Sundays were special. Every Sunday, my mother would create a menu, go shopping for ingredients, come home, and put together some of the most delicious meals I ever had. That was the birthplace of my food journey. I would watch her prep, put it all together, and then we would set the table, sit down, and have dinner together when it was all done.

Until this day, when I go home, my mom still makes Sunday dinners. Although I've learned most of the recipes and made them my own, I still watch her prep and put together our Sunday dinners as only as she can.

Nyska Merisier-Desarmes, Hair & Makeup Artist

▲ ▲

I love Haitian cuisine. I always wanted to open a restaurant. My favorite meal growing up was Diri Ak Pwa Vert (Rice with Green Peas). It's still one of my favorites. Now that my Mom is gone, I love eating her favorite meal (White Rice with White Bean Sauce). I also love Smoked Herring in Sauce with Boiled Plantains. I just love Haitian food!

Rachel Charles, Owner of Rachel's Sweet Confections

▲ ▲

As a kid, my favorite Haitian dish was Banan Peze and Griot with Pikliz. There was this one time when my family and I were on a summer vacation in Marigot (a suburb in Jacmel). We enjoyed eating delicious Haitian food every day.

Ed Gehy, Professor

▲▲▲▲▲▲▲▲▲▲▲▲▲▲▲▲▲▲▲▲▲▲▲▲▲▲▲▲

Everything about our culture is worthy of being preserved and passed on to the next generation. My favorite Haitian foods are: Griot ak Pikliz (Fried Pork with Coleslaw), Banan Peze (Fried Plantains), Zaboka (Avocado), Salad Leti-tomat (Lettuce-Tomato Salad), Diri Kole ak Pwa Rouj (Rice and Red Beans), and yon boutèy fwi kola (a bottle of Fruit Cola).

Dr. Mireille Lauture, Author

▲ ▲

Haitian food played a big role in bringing my family together. We always had so many great cooks, especially my mom. My most memorable time eating Haitian food has to be Thanksgiving. There's just so much! My favorite dishes are Potato Salad, Diri Kole ak Pwa Roug (Rice and Red Beans), Legim (Legumes), and so much more! I also love our soups – Bouyon, Doumbrey, and, of course, Soup Joumou (Pumpkin Soup).

Farrah M. J. Louis, Journalist

▲ ▲

Actually, I'm not Haitian – but after working so closely with Jean, I think I could count as an honorary Haitian! I love Akra (Taro Root Fritters) and Pikliz (Coleslaw) and so many other Haitian foods. I think Haitian food is one of the best cuisines in the world and one of Haiti's great treasures!

Stephanie Scherpf,
Executive Director of Jean Appolon Expressions (JAE)

▲ ▲

I am a vegetarian, and it's difficult to think of a Haitian dish that doesn't contain meat. My meals include a mixed salad, rice, and beans. I also like tropical fruits.

Joseph Makhandal Champagne, Attorney

▲ ▲

My most memorable time eating Haitian food is during parties. Although Haitian food is part of my daily diet, I know that there is something different about it - maybe, it is the garnish, or the cook puts a little more spice and extra love into it. All I know is that the food is always heavenly.

Marjorie Vail,
Teacher, Licensed Esthetician, and
Former Mrs. New York International 2015

▲ ▲

I love Fritay aka Fried Foods, i.e. Griot (Fried Pork), Banan Peze (Fried Plantains), etc. There's absolutely not a more adequate appetizer for me. There's never any guilt in eating these fried delights with a side of Pikliz (Coleslaw)!

I will never forget having Fritay on the beach the first time I went to Haiti. I've never witnessed anything quite like it. I thought it was a festival for that day because music was playing, and different things were being sold in the area. However, it was just a normal day in Port Salut. There was so much culture. I loved it!

Fabiola Jean, Journalist

▲ ▲

I had a lobster dish by the ocean in Haiti recently that was mind-blowing! I moved to the U.S., but I grew up in Haiti so I ate Haitian food every day. Whenever I visit Haiti, I savor every meal even more than before. My all-time favorites are Lalo, Griot, Pikliz, and Black Mushroom Rice. I also love Pwason Gwo Sel (Red Snapper).

Fabienne Sylvia Josaphat-Merritt, Author

▲ ▲

My favorite Haitian meal includes Black Mushroom Rice (Diri Djon-Djon), Beef, and Legim (Legumes). My favorite Haitian snacks are Beef or Chicken Patties (Patés). My most memorable time eating Haitian food was when my mom taught me how to make Patés from scratch and they were served at the party she was hosting.

Everyone found the food I had made extra delicious. I appreciated all that went into the preparation, but I was very proud to have my own labor as part of the offerings.

Ingrid Austin Daniels, Founder of
Cornbread and Cremasse Haitian-American Blog

▲ ▲

My favorite dish is Diri Djon-Djon. My mom makes it with shrimp. I also really like Fritay (Griot and Banan Peze) with some serious hot Pikliz.

My most memorable time eating Haitian food was during my first trip to Haiti. It was the mid-1990s, and I was a teenager. Back then, I wasn't into Haitian culture at all. In fact, I didn't even want to go on that trip. My family and I spent two weeks there, and the trip was absolutely amazing. The food was DIVINE! Not only was everything absolutely delicious, but we toured the country. Even when we went to eat at restaurants, everything tasted different, but in a good way.

We visited Port-au-Prince, Gonaïves, Cap Haitian, and the south. I got to experience the different regional dishes. Everything was super fresh. We often picked out the goat or pig that was to be dinner that night. The food was made with love.

There was one particular day that we were at my father's aunt's house in Gonaïves and she made Soup Joumou (Pumpkin Soup). To this day, I still haven't tasted a Soup Joumou that good!

Haitian food was really my introduction into Haitian culture. It was my way of becoming more aware and a part of my culture and heritage. Haitian food taught me how to love and appreciate Haiti and myself.

Melissa P. Bernier, Attorney

▲ ▲

I've always enjoyed eating Haitian food, but I fell in love with it in my pre-teen years. After tasting foods from many cultures, I realized that there was no flavor that can be compared to Haitian food.

Haitian food is unique, and I don't want to take it for granted. Although many islands prepare similar dishes, Haitian food has an acquired taste. Even the preparation of the spices make an impact on the authenticity of the meals. I've made an effort to learn everything that my mother knows about Haitian food so that my children can experience authentic Haitian meals!

Mohan Jean-Mary, Hairstylist at MODIMEL Studios

▲▲▲▲▲▲▲▲▲▲▲▲▲▲▲▲▲▲▲▲▲▲▲▲▲

I love Haitian food. I don't really have a particular favorite dish, but I must tell you that plantains are used in every special dish in Haiti. I personally like to prepare plantains in many different ways. I boil them, I fry them, and so on.

We also have different types of plantains that we grow in Haiti. For instance, we have po ban, miske, ponyak, fig dous, and fig sale. Po ban is a very important plantain in Haiti. It is known for good and substantial nutrients which satisfy hunger quickly, and strengthen the muscles and the bones.

Huguens Mercier, Author

▲▲▲▲▲▲▲▲▲▲▲▲▲▲▲▲▲▲▲▲▲▲▲▲▲▲

In fact, Haitian food can be very healthy! I'm a vegetarian. I love Legim (Legumes), Igname (yams), and anything that comes from the ground. I love Salad Zaboka (Avocado Salad). I also love Diri Djon-Djon. All Haitians love Black Mushroom Rice!

As a child, we used to eat a lot of Mayi Moulen (Cornmeal) with Sòs Pwa Nwa (Black Bean Sauce), but I only loved the sauce. Actually, I remember when I wasn't gaining weight after having my son, and someone suggested that I should drink Sòs Pwa because I needed iron. I actually did re-gain the weight!

Elsie Chery, Social Worker

▲ ▲

Haitian food is very healthy because we take time to cook it. I like all kinds of Haitian food. I don't have any particular favorite meal, but I like my chicken and I like my black rice. I love the spices as well.

Alix Chery, Realtor

▲▲▲▲▲▲▲▲▲▲▲▲▲▲▲▲▲▲▲▲▲▲▲▲▲▲

I enjoy Haitian cuisine for its bold flavors. I often eat rice and beans with Legim (Legumes), Soup Joumou (Pumpkin Soup), even Akra (Taro Fritters), or plantains with Pikliz (Coleslaw).

I love Haitian cuisine, primarily because it's a part of my culture. It's what I know and can appreciate because of our struggles and resilient spirit. We love to cook. We love family, and food is a great way to bring and keep people together.

Kristia Beaubrun, Public Relations Professional

▲ ▲

On most Sundays mornings, after walking home with my sister from church, the smell of my grandmother's cooking would greet us at the gate before reaching her doorsteps. She knew that our favorite dish was Chaka.

I remember my grandmother slowly stirring the stew for long periods of time so that it won't burn to the bottom of the pot. She would pass over the big wooden spoon so that my sister and I would take turns stirring. It was a meal that required patience and love.

At that time, there was no prettier sight than a plate loaded with Chaka: Fresh Garlic, Corn, Red Beans, and Smoked Pork topped with Parsley. Over the years, I've yet to find a stew made in the same way as my grandmother's. Thinking of it now makes me want to run to her house!

Tracy Guiteau, Artist and Fashion Designer

44

▲▲▲▲▲▲▲▲▲▲▲▲▲▲▲▲▲▲▲▲▲▲▲▲▲▲

Banan+Griot+Pikliz = Heaven.

I really like Fritay!

All plantains and Griot (Fried Pork) taste the same, but the magic is in the Pikliz (Coleslaw). It's where the Fritay wins or fails. The best one I've ever had was in Jacmel. I had bought it from the last woman in the row of street vendors. It was so good! Sometimes, I just wanted a jar of the Pikliz, but they never wanted to sell it to me.

I also love Diri Djon-Djon with some Piskett (those super small fishes that you find in the Jacmel area). During my childhood, the electricity usually came back on around 8pm. From the end of the school day until the next day, I had nothing to do. My friends and I used to cook Lam Veritab (Breadfruit).

I remember I made a hot sauce so hot that every guy who tried it was sweating even though there was a nice breeze! There was this one time, we were at the beach. After cooking the Lam Veritab, some of the guys threw some of it from a cliff, and we had to dive and swim to get it. Those were fun times.

A few years ago, I was in New York with some friends, and I wanted them to have an opportunity to taste Haitian food. I spent a nice chunk of change for some rice and beans and Fritay. I had this Korean friend who took a piece of fat off from the Griot, and he asked, "Is this a piece of fat?" I answered, "Yeah!"

Then, he ate it, and said, "It's so good!" I looked at him dumbfounded, and thought, "In Haiti, the street

45

vendors get yelled at for giving you pieces of fat and here is this guy, and he just loves it!" Sak pa bon pou youn, pi bon pou yon lot! (One man's trash is another's treasure!)

Olivier Duong, Photographer

▲▲▲▲▲▲▲▲▲▲▲▲▲▲▲▲▲▲▲▲▲▲▲▲▲

I'll say that my all-time favorite Haitian meal is Diri Blan with Sòs Pwa Nwa (White Rice with Black Bean Sauce) and Legim (Legumes). My mom would make huge pots of each and we would fill our plates. Then, other family members would come over and eat!

I always questioned, "Why are they eating our food?" However, my mom was a giver, and she always cooked her food - always providing for as many as she could and not just for her family. I now try to do the same.

Jessica Descartes, Educator

47

▲ ▲

I would have to say that my favorite Haitian food would have to be Griot and Diri Djon-Djon (Black Mushroom Rice). Hands down. I don't know what my mom does to make it so good, but I applaud her each time!

Alexandra Josephine Morquette,
Co-President of the Columbia University
Haitian Students' Association

▲ ▲

My favorite dish is Diri Djon-Djon and Griot. I also love Pwason Salé (saltfish) with yams and plantains.

Seven years ago, before I left Haiti, my grandmother prepared that for my family, and it was so good. Since then, I never had a good Pwason Salé. I think it's because I can't find good saltfish as the ones in Haiti!

Medjy Mezilus, Fashion Designer

My memory of eating Haitian food is a recent one at my dad's repass. Family and friends were gathered, and I tasted my cousin's rice which I hadn't had in about 15 years. Because of the age difference, she was more like an aunt than a cousin.

"Ki-sa ou vle manje?" my cousin asked me. "What do you want to eat?"

Her food always hit the spot. She used sweeter seasoning on her rice; and, of course, the pot was filled with red kidney beans. Just smelling it unlocked old memories, and tasting it unlocked even more.

I suddenly remembered a game of musical chairs from more than a decade ago. I remembered being forced into playing "house" with my cousins who were all girls. I also remembered my First Communion. That era of my childhood was the one where I picked up most of the Haitian Creole that I know.

Romel Edmond, Writer

▲ ▲

Lambi (Stewed Conch) is my favorite. Whenever I had the opportunity to enjoy Lambi nan Sòs (Conch in Sauce), it was during either a communion, wedding, or celebration. It marked a time of a special occasion, and festivity with family and close friends. The two together will always be so healing – the true definition of "soul food."

Florcy Morisset,
Founder & Director of Vivant Art Collection

▲▲▲▲▲▲▲▲▲▲▲▲▲▲▲▲▲▲▲▲▲▲▲▲▲

I love Pen Patate.

Berlotte Antoine, Radio Host

▲▲▲▲▲▲▲▲▲▲▲▲▲▲▲▲▲▲▲▲▲▲▲▲▲▲▲▲

When my sisters and I were younger, our parents would fill our plates with a lot of food (especially with all the things we hated). They would tell us we couldn't move from the table until our plates were cleaned. One Sunday, my mom made white rice and peas alongside turkey and sauce. It was a simple meal, but as a picky eater, I disliked turkey.

Sitting in front of my plate, I wondered, "Why didn't my mom cook Poul Di (Hen) and Sòs Pwa (Bean Sauce)? I totally would have finished that meal in a matter of seconds." One by one, I watched as all my sisters finished their meals and scattered to enjoy the rest of the day while I sat sunken in my chair, picking at my food.

As my mom cleaned the dishes, she kept saying phrases like "Hurry up" and "Eat, Daphnie, so you can grow." Half an hour later, my mom finished the dishes, and came and sat next to me. Like a baby, she forced-fed me the turkey and the rest of my meal. This memory is one that will forever stay etched in my memory as one of my earliest picky eater-isms while growing up in a Haitian family.

Daphnie Bordes, Writer/Blogger

▲ ▲

I love mushroom rice and fried plantains. My most memorable moment was at a restaurant in Haiti. I was with good friends, and the food was freshly prepared. Although I'm not a fish lover, the red snapper was amazing.

Esther Simon, Parent

▲ ▲

My favorite meal is Akasan. It's a form of porridge. I am always reminded of my childhood when I have Akasan!

During the early weekend mornings, there would be this lady selling it in my neighborhood (Pernier), or a family friend would make the best in town. Having it in the early mornings with warm Haitian bread and peanut butter made everything seem alright. The taste, the smell, and the color made you take your time to savor every spoonful.

Debbie Jean-Jacques, Student

▲ ▲

I love Bouyon (Soup). I come from the mountains. We live near the sea, and we always drink pure water. I love Sòs Pwa (Bean Sauce) because it has a lot of vitamins, irons, and protein. I also love my green plantains.

Lucie Monestime, Patient Care Technician

▲ ▲

Food is one of those things that factor into the fondest of memories. I recall swapping sandwiches and desserts with classmates in Haiti. I remember my family taking us to Osai Kai, the premier Chinese restaurant in Port-au-Prince. I think about having sushi in Philadelphia with a friend; lox at the Four Seasons in D.C.; filet mignon at The Plaza; and, late night black rice at La Caye in Brooklyn.

Patriotic Pumpkin Soup on New Year's Day occupies centerstage in my heart. I make it numerous times a year, especially in winter. Back home, it was a perennial ritual to clean the treasured Copeland Spode blue and white china from my mother's mahogany cabinet. The china had been a gift from a wealthy neighbor of Syrian descent.

Next to my mother's delicious soup, one of the most memorable meals I had took place recently. A group of us were on our way to a festival in Aquin, Haiti. Somehow, I had the chance to be with a few of my favorite musicians. The bus carrying us rocked with laughter from jokes and anticipation. We got to know one another through the stories we told. We sang; musicians drummed on the seats, and played air guitar.

When hunger's sting became unbearable, we stopped to eat at the food stalls framing the road. Before we could exit the bus, the vendors charged toward us with tasty morsels. "Try my food." "Eat here." "My price is better than his." On and on the competition went. What the vendors didn't know was we were too hungry to care about *price or anything else. If it was edible, we were ready to ingest it.*

We bought platters heaped with fried plantains, Griot, rice and beans, Pikliz - the works! We ate with our fingers, and chatted with strangers. The food was fantastic! The grilled conch tasted like a dream. The musicians drew quite a crowd of fans and curious eyes. It was a great memory in the making. Just beyond the food stalls was the blue-blue Caribbean Sea, which seemed to enhance the meal's flavor. When we reached Aquin, we met with more musicians, laughed, and ate some more.

The morning after the concert found us in a quaint hotel that had prepared a special breakfast for the musicians. It was not my mother's pumpkin soup, but it won second place! So many famous musicians were there, behaving like normal folks - getting scolded by family members for having "overdone it" the previous night.

While we ate, one of my biggest dreams came true. Some of the musicians stood to greet a "personage." Danny Laférièrre happened to be there, having breakfast with his family. I almost imploded with excitement. I had one more reason to count Pumpkin Soup as one of my top five meals. Again, it had more to do with people than the actual food.

Katia D. Ulysse, Author

58

▲ ▲

My favorite Haitian dish is Tomtom ak Kalalou. It's a staple dish from my hometown in Les Cayes (south of Haiti). I also like Legim (Legumes), Griot, Fried Plantains, Diri Djon-Djon, White Rice with Sòs Pwa, and Poul nan Sòs.

During Reveillon on Christmas Eve and after Midnight Mass, we have Sòs Pwa Congo, White Rice, and Lambi. On January 1st, we always have Soup Joumou.

Mary Leon Bourjolly, Educator

▲ ▲

Some of my favorite Haitian dishes are Diri, Sòs Pwa, and Legim (Legumes). I also love Diri Djon-Djon, which is one of my specialties. When my friends are planning for parties, they always ask me to prepare that dish for them. I love to cook. It's not a chore for me. People may not realize it, but I can cook up a storm!

Margarette Tropnas, Community Activist

▲ ▲

I love different types of Haitian food, but what brings the most memories is Soup Joumou. As a kid, both my mom and grandma would stay up late on New Year's Eve to make it. It's such a celebratory time, and all of us get to help out!

Lorraine A. Charles, Medical Professional
& Mrs. Haiti International 2014

▲▲▲▲▲▲▲▲▲▲▲▲▲▲▲▲▲▲▲▲▲▲▲▲

I love a well-cooked Haitian meal. As a proud Haitian, I cannot spend a week without eating Haitian food. In my family, there is a tradition where each day, we cook a specific meal. I have three favorite days: Saturday (Corn, Fish, or Blé [Bulgar Wheat]); Wednesday (Legumes); and, Friday (Bouyon).

On Wednesdays, we eat Lalo which is spinach. I am a Gonaivien so this has been my favorite food since I was a young boy. Not everyone knows how to cook Lalo. My second favorite is Bouyon. It is very comforting and healthy. I am from a family of fashionistas and doctors; therefore, eating healthy to remain slim is a must. We avoid the spicy foods and anything with lots of fat. We do not eat red meat, pork, or steak.

My most memorable Haitian meal is drinking Soup Joumou on January 1st. There is a sense of pride from everyone, and seeing all of us together is mesmerizing.

Ciano Clerjuste, Founder,
Chairman & President of United Colors of Fashion

▲▲▲▲▲▲▲▲▲▲▲▲▲▲▲▲▲▲▲▲▲▲▲▲▲▲▲

In my family, food is a very important matter. My mother is a real "Cordon Bleu" and has transformed the way people look at Haitian food. My favorite dish is Krab ak Berejenn (Crab with Eggplant), Diri Blan ak Pwa Blan (White Rice with White Beans), Pwason Gwo Sèl (Red Snapper), and Poul Kreyol (Haitian Chicken).

I remember when my family and I were in Kenscoff, Haiti. My mother prepared Diri Kole ak Pwa (Rice and Beans). She cooked the rice with some ham she had prepared the day before. She fried the Pwa (Beans) and put them on top of the rice! I remember the Poul Peyi (Hen) that she made with it. We also had dessert - Blan Manje (Haitian Fruit Cocktail).

Yanick J.P. Lahens, Author

▲▲▲▲▲▲▲▲▲▲▲▲▲▲▲▲▲▲▲▲▲▲▲▲▲

I love Banan Peze (Fried Plantains) with Lambi (Conch). I also love Diri Kole (Rice and Beans), Diri Djon-Djon (Black Mushroom Rice), and Cabrit Boucane (Grilled Goat). I love to eat and savor Haitian food with my family and good friends over good conversations as we reminisce about Haiti.

Dr. Evelyn Julmisse, Educator

▲▲▲▲▲▲▲▲▲▲▲▲▲▲▲▲▲▲▲▲▲▲▲▲▲

My favorite Haitian dishes are Boulette (Meatballs), Legim (Legumes), and Makawoni au Graten (Macaroni and Cheese). These make me think back to family holidays when there was a table full of these dishes plus lots more. I would start at one end with an empty plate and leave the other end with the most delicious combination of my favorite dishes. The meals were always made with so much flavor and love.

Yamilee Toussaint, Educator

▲ ▲

My favorite Haitian dishes include Soup Joumou (Pumpkin Soup), Tassot (Fried Goat), Makawoni au Graten (Macaroni and Cheese), and Salade Russe. In particular, Soup Joumou holds very special memories for me. Soup Joumou represents the New Year and our Independence Day, not to mention the opportunity to bring family together to celebrate.

From Midnight Masses to ring in the New Year to sharing a bowl of Soup Joumou in every Haitian household you visit on January 1st, it is powerful to see how a dish can continue to have both historical and social significance among Haitians - not to mention the labor of love that goes into all the ingredient prep and cooking of Soup Joumou!

Nedgine Paul Deroly,
Co-founder & CEO Anseye Pou Ayiti (Teach for Haiti)

▲ ▲

Some of my favorite Haitian foods are Mayi Moulen (Cornmeal) with Aransò (Herring) and avocado; Diri Djon-Djon (Black Mushroom Rice) with crab; and, Bouyon (Soup). My favorite dessert is Ambrosia (Fruit Cocktail). My most memorable times of eating Haitian food were during family events when they became potlucks. Relatives would bring their specialty dishes, and we would break bread together.

Dina Simon,
Founder and Managing Director of My Haiti Travels

▲ ▲

My favorite Haitian meals are Legim (Legumes), Diri Blan, and Soup Joumou. I can eat them every day and be happy. I learned how to make Soup Joumou only a few years ago! I love it! I can't make Legim (Legumes) yet but that's next on my list.

Wanda Tima-Gilles, Founder of L'Union Suite

▲ ▲

I love that Haitian food bursts with mouth-watering spices and bold zesty flavor. Let's not even talk about the seductive aromas which escape out of a Kreyol kitchen's window. It can be a seaside blend: Lambi (conch), lobster, shrimp, crab, snapper, cod, or erring. It might be chicken, goat, pork and turkey. You may find root vegetables like yams, potatoes, Manyok (tapioc), carrots, and beets. Whatever are the cook's pick of ingredients, it is the blending of fresh herbs, vegetables, spices, and marinades in a slow-roasted, slow-cooked way that brings it all together.

I absolutely love that Haitians use a pilon (pestle and mortar) to crush parsley leaves, Scotch Bonnet Peppers, and vegetables, which releases the aromatic oils and maximizes the natural flavors. The food is prepared with lots of love and care that you can really savor. It's good food for the soul. Some of my personal favorites are Ragu ak Diri Blan (Pig's Feet with White Rice), Poul ak Nwa, Legumes, Black Rice with Tassot, and the salty/sweet and crispy Plantains with a side of Pikliz!

One of the most memorable times was visiting my grandparents in Cap-Haitien and always smelling something comforting and familiar wafting from their kitchen. They would always let me snack on breadfruits or help snap some peas. I even remember seeing the crabs moving around in the pot when I was six years old. Cap-Haitien is known for its stew chicken with cashews – a dish I still favor to this day.

Myriam Jean, Educator

69

▲▲▲▲▲▲▲▲▲▲▲▲▲▲▲▲▲▲▲▲▲▲▲▲▲▲

As a child, I was transported into a world of rich culinary tradition every time I spent time with my grandmother in the kitchen. Patat ak Let (Sweet Potato with Milk) was a lot different compared to a nice bowl of cereal, but once I had a taste, it became one of my favorite things to eat. I've experienced this feeling many times, mostly when I eat a dish that my grandmother used to make. My grandmother was the best cook to ever walk the Earth.

Carmel Balan, Founder of Port Academie

▲ ▲

I love Diri Kole ak Pwa Congo (Rice with Pigeon Peas), Legim (Legumes), and Lambi. My favorite time eating Haitian food is always at gatherings or family affairs. Food makes people happy. It brings laughter and warmth, and it's the best feeling in the world. If you have ever been to a Haitian party with all the Haitian Food, you're guaranteed to have a good time and your stomach will most definitely be full.

Lulu Orange Tyson, Nurse & Mrs. Haiti International 2016

▲ ▲

Two of my favorite Haitian meals are Bouyon and Diri Djon-Djon. My mother made Bouyon every Saturday, and our trip to the local vegetable market was very special. My favorite memory is gathering with the neighbors in the backyard. I remember all of the laughter. We were really happy – it was the real joie de vivre.

Paulette Salisbury, Chef

▲ ▲

Some of my favorite Haitian meals are:

1. Diri Djon-Djon (Black Mushroom Rice)
2. Mayi Moulen ak Zaboka (Cornmeal with Avocado)
3. Soup Joumou (Pumpkin Soup)
4. Lambi (Conch)

My most memorable time eating Haitian food is eating it in Haiti. Sometimes, on Haitian beaches, the fisherman will sell you a fish and someone will grill it for you right there. Or, they will grill newly caught Lambi and dip it in Pikliz. It's the best Haitian food I've ever eaten.

Edwidge Danticat, Author

73

▲ ▲

I consider myself an honorary Haitian. Last year, I worked alongside an organization and we were hosting a Haitian concert. Our contract required that we provide food to the artists that evening. I had never eaten Haitian food, and I thought I would refrain because I was going to be very busy that evening.

All of the work I did created an appetite. An hour before the show, I snuck to the kitchen and fixed a plate with chicken patties, beans and rice, and some pink-colored medley that looked like potato salad. The pink thing - I can't recall what it was, BLEW MY MIND! It was SO good that I kept going back to get more of it. The patties were excellent. As the project manager, I was waving around directions with one hand while happily eating a patty with the other.

Charlotte Clark, Environmental Consultant

▲▲▲▲▲▲▲▲▲▲▲▲▲▲▲▲▲▲▲▲▲▲▲▲▲▲

Our rich, flavorful Haitian food is one of the many treasures we get to experience in our culture. I absolutely love Beyens (Banana Fritters). The sweet banana fried dough is delicious and addictive. Although it is popular during carnivals, one can also find them throughout the year. Whenever I am in Haiti, I make it a point to visit some of my favorite street food vendors to complete the sense of being home.

Daniella Bien-Aime, Founder of Bien-Aime Post

▲▲▲▲▲▲▲▲▲▲▲▲▲▲▲▲▲▲▲▲▲▲▲▲▲▲▲

Legume Krab ak Lambi with white rice has a special place in my heart. I grew up in a single-father household, and my dad is an awesome cook. He knew how much I loved Legumes.

So, whenever he punished me for something and wanted to show remorse, the next day I would find the upper echelon of all Legim (Legumes) – Legim adorned with my favorite seafood: crab and conch. The Legim was served with the grainiest and tastiest of white rice. The white rice was spiced with just a piece of fried scallion and two cloves of garlic seasoned with salt. Nothing tasted better.

Nadege Fleurimond, Author & Chef

▲ ▲

My favorite Haitian meals are Legumes with White Rice or Diri Djon-Djon. I also love AK-100 (aka Akasan) and Labouyi (Porridge). My most memorable time eating Haitian food was when we visited family in Miami and New York and just hung out in the kitchen while my family cooked and told jokes.

Denice Chinn, Entrepreneur

▲ ▲

When I lived in Haiti over a decade ago, my mom had a tradition where she would cook white rice with Legim (Legumes) and white kidney beans gravy. I used to get so excited when the weekends came around. I knew Sunday would come, and I would get to eat this wonderful dish. My mom would also make fried fish; or, sometimes switch it up with fried chicken. We always had beet potato salad on the side. It was all so delicious!

Rebecca Alfred, Educator

▲ ▲

My favorite Haitian dish is Mayi Moulen (Cornmeal Porridge) with Black Beans and Legim (Legumes). I lived in Port-au-Prince, but when school was closed, I would stay at my grandmother's house in Jacmel. Those were some of my best memories because her food was heavenly.

Agathina Nozy, Student

▲ ▲

My favorite Haitian food is Fritay (Fried Foods). For me, Fritay is associated with family and community. Growing up in Haiti, my sisters, cousins, and I were only allowed to eat Fritay on Fridays. I also remember when relatives and the children from the neighborhood would sit on our front yard and look up at the stars at nighttime. We would talk and tell jokes before we went to sleep.

Fedia Louis, Social Worker

▲▲▲▲▲▲▲▲▲▲▲▲▲▲▲▲▲▲▲▲▲▲▲▲▲

My favorite Haitian food is a delicacy – Pikliz. I love the taste. The spicier, the better. It is a wonder because it could make unsweetened, hard, and crispy plantains taste like heaven. I could eat Pikliz with meat, or just by itself.

Errold Moy Michel, Medical Logistics Officer

▲ ▲

I have fond memories of my family making Griot (Fried Pork), Diri Djon-Djon (Black Mushroom Rice), and Banan Peze (Fried Plantains) for every special celebration we had.

Sabene Similien, Administrator

▲ ▲

My favorite Haitian dish is Marinad (Fritters) and Fritay (Fried Foods) – not necessarily because of an affinity for the taste, but for the memories I have associated with these tasty treats. I remember strolling the streets of Port-au-Prince every summer with my gang of cousins, after our grandmother distributed money between the six of us.

We'd look for our favorite food merchant, and wait anxiously as she deep fried the fritters. Those moments, surrounded by my cousins as we walked back home, eating our flavorful treats and laughing amongst ourselves, are some of my favorite memories.

Vania André, Editor-in-Chief of The Haitian Times

83

▲ ▲

More than a necessary physical need, Haitian food is the pillar of my very being. When I eat Diri Blan, Sòs Pwa with Toufe Legumes or with Beregèn ak Lambi and Krab, goat meat with Diri ak Pwa Kole (our national rice), or Mayi Moulen ak Aransò and Zaboka, I'm taken back to my childhood in the motherland. Eating those dishes that nourished my ancestors links me to spiritual and traditional acts which reveal the culture and history of Haiti which define me.

When I visit family in Haiti or in New York, I am like a hungry baby eager to be breastfed by a mother. Nothing is more gratifying than eating Haitian food. Even though my travels and experiences have exposed me to a wide variety of cuisine that I enjoy, no other food can touch my soul deeper than authentic Haitian cuisine; it seals the continuity of my past and present lives.

However, I must confess that my own cooking is an amalgam of the various cultures I have experienced. I love to explore and experiment in the kitchen. I unscrupulously alter or add ingredients to surprise my palate. I am, therefore, unfaithful in the kitchen, totally unable to create the exact same dish in the same manner. Yet, the Haitian influence in my cooking is undeniable. I am what I cook.

Elsie Augustave, Author

▲▲▲▲▲▲▲▲▲▲▲▲▲▲▲▲▲▲▲▲▲▲▲▲▲▲

My favorites are Makawoni au Graten (Macaroni and Cheese), Griot, Tassot Cabrit (Fried Goat), and Black Rice. Some of my absolute favorite Haitian foods are white rice, red bean soup, and Legim (Legumes). I have a lot of people over for Thanksgiving and Christmas, and we share lots of laughs!

Lynnsie Augustin, Entrepreneur

▲ ▲

During the summertime, my parents used to send us to Haiti to spend time with our grandmother in Aux Cayes (south of Port-au-Prince). It wasn't unusual for my grandmother to have at least 27 grandchildren with her. We pretty much occupied the whole town.

I remember the time we all went to our uncle's house. It was a feast. They killed many animals for dinner, and they cooked a lot of food for all of us. We ate lots of fruits such as watermelon, mangos, etc. The beauty of it all is that all of the food came from the family's farms.

When we returned to Grandma's place, she asked, "Are you guys full?" We responded, "Yes." Then, she jokingly said, "Well, you guys ate for three days, and I'm not cooking at all for the remainder of the week!"

Andrea Graham, Mrs. Haiti International 2015

▲▲▲▲▲▲▲▲▲▲▲▲▲▲▲▲▲▲▲▲▲▲▲▲▲▲▲▲

From Griot to Legim (Legumes) to Lalo, it's nearly impossible for me to choose one favorite dish from Haitian cuisine. Diri ak Sòs Pwa (Rice with Bean Sauce), however, is a dish that brings many happy childhood memories.

I remember coming home from school, and putting away my uniform and bookbag. I sat at the table and waited for a warm plate of rice and bean sauce. It really didn't matter if there was any kind of meat accompanying it. I couldn't wait to mix my rice with the velvety soup-like beans. The main attraction was really the Sòs Pwa; the rice was there just to add texture.

After filling my hungry belly with Diri ak Sòs Pwa, and ignoring whatever piece of meat it came with, I would turn on the TV and watch cartoons while sipping on a tall glass of lemonade. To this day, I always serve myself proportionally less rice than beans.

Maureen Boyer, Author

▲ ▲

Mayi Moulen reminds me of my grandmother's cooking. It was simple, filling, and full of love - just like her. As a child, I could care less about eating it. I had no choice. However, this dish brings a longing for her, and for other loved ones I've lost since she passed away. The memory of it pushes me to treasure my mother, who's still with us. She used to force us to eat it because it was good for us - it was Haitian, and yes, she made it and that was that.

Myriam-Skye Holly, Writer & Educator

▲ ▲

One of my favorite Haitian meals includes Legim (Legumes) with any kind of Sòs Pwa (Bean Sauce) and Mayi Moulen (Corn Meal Porridge). It was the absolute favorite thing I would enjoy eating with my grandmother, Liliane, while watching Soul Train on TV on Saturdays. She was an excellent cook, and I could always taste the love. That's an ingredient I always want to add in the meals I cook and share with others. You can always taste the love in Haitian food . . . from beginning to end.

Daphne Ferdinand, Founder of the
The New York School of Protocol and Etiquette

▲ ▲

I never really liked Diri ak Sòs Pwa (Rice with Bean Sauce) as a kid. But, now it has become one of my favorite dishes, especially with some Poul nan Sòs on top. It's great for Saturday's, but not for Sunday's after church. On Sunday, my mother, aunt, or grandmother usually showed off their culinary skills.

For Sunday, there was the Banan Peze with watercress, dabbled with some sauce on top and some Pikliz on the side. Then, there was the potato salad with the beets. Yes, they put some sauce on that, too. Then, there was the Diri Kole with Legim (Legumes), preferably made of eggplants, lots of spinach, and carrots.

Josue Pierre,
Democratic State Committeeman/District Leader

▲ ▲

My favorite meal is Bouyon. I was a picky eater when I was younger. Whenever my mom made Bouyon, I got excited because I had a ton of options to eat from, such as the dumplings, plantains, sweet potatoes, etc. The dumplings were the best parts. My mom had a way of making them. They were small and soft. Bouyon is still my favorite meal.

Claudine Mondesir, Entrepreneur

▲ ▲

I love Haitian food. I live for Haitian food. The culture that exudes from the food is telling in the heart of the one who made it. My favorite dish is Legim (Legumes). It's the kind of dish that, if made correctly, will touch your whole soul! Just talking about it excites my taste buds.

Tracey F. Laroche, Philanthropist

▲▲▲▲▲▲▲▲▲▲▲▲▲▲▲▲▲▲▲▲▲▲▲▲

Marinad (Fritters) bring back memories of my First Communion. It was the first thing I ate when I came home from the church. My dad's hit song, *"Premiere Communion,"* with the group, Bossa Combo, was playing in the background. I remember my aunt and grandmother were in the kitchen, seasoning the flour, adding the meat, rolling it with their hands, and dropping it in the pan to fry. I loved fried food as a kid. That remains as one of the best memories I had because of the people that were in the kitchen that day.

I've never had anything quite like Lambi here in the States. I usually dress it with a little pikliz before I dive in. It's the best feeling to be on the beach somewhere in Haiti, eating freshly caught seafood with fried plantains and drinking a cold bottle of Prestige!

My favorite dish of all time is Legim (Legumes). My grandmother always made it with such love that came from the depths of her soul. Legim is an authentically Haitian food. It's packed with greens/veggies, and an array of meats. You can add seafood to it. You can even have it vegan style! Top it off with a side of white rice and Sòs Pwa makes it the ultimate Haitian comfort food.

Soraya Denis Volcy, Founder & CEO of Dlo Pou Viv

▲▲▲▲▲▲▲▲▲▲▲▲▲▲▲▲▲▲▲▲▲▲▲▲▲▲

I enjoyed eating Haitian food at home; my grandmother and mother cooked. I taught myself how to cook certain foods by watching them and reading a Haitian cookbook.

Stacey Toussaint, President & CEO of Inside Out Tours

▲▲▲▲▲▲▲▲▲▲▲▲▲▲▲▲▲▲▲▲▲▲▲▲▲▲▲▲

I love Griot, and I can eat it any time of the day with rice and red beans.

Naomie Dieduonne, Entrepreneur

▲▲▲▲▲▲▲▲▲▲▲▲▲▲▲▲▲▲▲▲▲▲▲▲▲▲▲▲

As a native Haitian, I have enjoyed a variety of Haitian food, but I have developed a particular affinity for rice mixed with red beans and Legim (Legumes), white rice and black beans puree, goat meat with sauce, Griot with fried green plantains, and Pikliz. Last but not least, I also enjoy Mayi Moulen and Black Bean Sauce with avocados.

Paul Celicourt, Entrepreneur

▲ ▲

My favorite Haitian dish is definitely goat with Dire Kole in sauce. For the longest time, I would say to my mom, "Make that special 'chicken' that I like." I didn't know it was goat until I was in my teens.

Whenever I was sick, my mom always gave me Labouyi Avwan ak Canel (Oatmeal Porridge with Cinnamon) and evaporated milk. She was insistent I had to eat it to regain my strength.

As an adult, there is nothing I enjoy more than being on the beach in Haiti and having fresh lobster with Pikliz, fried plantains, and a bottle of Prestige while laughing and spending time with those I love.

Yve-Car Momperousse,
Founder & CEO of Kreyol Essence

▲▲▲▲▲▲▲▲▲▲▲▲▲▲▲▲▲▲▲▲▲▲▲▲▲▲

I love Lambi, Mayi Moulen ak Sòs Pwa, Griot, and Tassot (Fried Goat); and, of course, Banan Peze. I love Pikliz. I also love Diri Djon-Djon and Soup Joumou.

My greatest memory of Haitian food was when I was in my early 20s. Back then, people used to have private little restaurants in their kitchens where they would just cook for your guests and you.

One Friday afternoon, at one of these restaurants, I was sitting with my uncle, Toto Mendes. (His family lived in Italy, but he's 100% pure Haitian.) We only spoke in Haitian Creole. We started eating and drinking at 1pm, and didn't stop until around 6pm. We ate a lot of food. We had everything - Lambi, Diri Djon-Djon, etc. I believe we had Griot, too.

We drank a full bottle of Rhum Barbancourt. As a testament to the quality and taste of Haitian food, I didn't even get a buzz from the rum. I didn't have a hangover. I didn't even feel heavy. Eating with my uncle at this woman's little restaurant in her home was a once-in-a-lifetime experience. It was purely a transformative experience, and I left that place feeling like I was truly Haitian - 100% Haitian.

Dr. Jeff Gardere, Psychologist

▲▲▲▲▲▲▲▲▲▲▲▲▲▲▲▲▲▲▲▲▲▲▲▲▲▲▲

I love Legim (Legumes) with rice and peas.

Jean Aluc, Student

▲ ▲

My absolute favorite Haitian food is Diri Kole ak Pwa (Rice and Beans). When I was a little girl, my mom prepared it. I love the process of boiling the beans, cutting the onions and garlic, and then sautéing the beans. The smell was aromatic and filled the entire house.

Culturally, I felt I was Haitian - I ate the food and spoke the language, but I didn't get to know it for myself until about two years ago when I had the opportunity to live and work in Haiti.

During my short time there, I felt as though I was one with the people. I was blown away when I discovered that the Diri Kole ak Pwa that I had as a child was also known as "Diri National" - the national dish in Haiti. Learning that, made this dish more special to me. It was then that I felt more connected to my roots.

I don't know who said it, but there's a quote I often say: "I am not Haitian because I was born in Haiti; I am Haitian because Haiti was born in me." The experience of being a Haitian woman is something that needs to be preserved and cherished. It's something intangible, but it is manifested by way of food, culture, and things of that nature.

Vanessa Leon,
Urban Planning & Public Policy Consultant

▲▲▲▲▲▲▲▲▲▲▲▲▲▲▲▲▲▲▲▲▲▲▲▲▲

Some of my favorite Haitian foods are Diri Blan, Sòs Pwa Rouj, ak Poul Di (White Rice, Red Bean Sauce, and Chicken).

When I was 16 or 17 years old, I was upset with my parents for some reason, and I decided to run away from home to "teach them a lesson." It was a Sunday. In most Haitian households, the best meals are cooked on Sundays. It's probably because that's the day most family members get together after church, and friends come to visit. In any case, I was so upset with my parents that I decided to run away.

I remember going to the kitchen to get a bag to put my stuff. I then noticed my mom cooking Diri Blan and Sòs Pwa Rouj. The minute I saw that I said to myself, "OK. I will stay home and run away next week." The silly things we say and do as children! I still cook this meal on most Sundays as an adult!

Another good Haitian meal that I have acquired a taste for is Lalo ak Diri Blan (Jute Leaves with White Rice) - a favorite for people from Gonaïves Latibonit. My husband is from Gonaïves, and he loves this dish so much. As a Haitian American, I had to learn how to cook this meal. I am happy to say that I also learned how to cook many other Haitian meals.

Susie Pepe, Founder & Chairman of
Pass the Torch Foundation, Inc.

▲ ▲

My favorite Haitian foods are Diri Djon-Djon with Shrimp, and Banan Peze with Griot.

I remember going to Port Salut when I was younger. I was eating Tomtom ak Kalalou Gombo (Breadfruit with Okra), but I couldn't eat it properly. To eat it properly is to swallow it in one go, but I could not do that no matter how hard I tried. My family members always teased me about the fact that I had to chew it before I swallowed it.

Garland Viaud, Graphic Designer

▲▲▲▲▲▲▲▲▲▲▲▲▲▲▲▲▲▲▲▲▲▲▲▲▲▲▲

I love Tarte a L'oignon (Onion Pie), a dish inspired by French cuisine. It is mostly consumed in Port-au-Prince and is not a typical Haitian dish. I love Legim (Legumes) (vegetables, eggplant with crabs, conch, and beef) with white rice and white bean sauce. I love Black Rice with Poul Peyi (Haitian chicken meat that is close to hen). I also love potato salad, fried plantains, and Bouyon (vegetable stew) with goat meat. I have a special place in my heart for porridge especially Mayi Moulen (made with corn meal) and Akasan (made with corn flour).

Since I grew up in Haiti, I have innumerable memories of eating Haitian food. But I would say that having my aunt and my grandmother cook sweet cornmeal has been a memorable experience. Since my grandmother passed, my aunt remains the only other person in my family who knows how to cook the cornmeal the way that I love it. She is the only one with my grandmother's recipe.

I have fond memories visiting family and friends in the countryside. They always cooked the food with lots of love. It's always a communal effort where many people get involved. They get some of the ingredients right off their gardens.

I used to enjoy going up to the mountains in Kenscoff with friends to buy street food - mostly plantains and Griot (pork). It was always an amazing time and it was the most delicious Griot in town.

Stephanie Senat, Humanitarian

▲▲▲▲▲▲▲▲▲▲▲▲▲▲▲▲▲▲▲▲▲▲▲▲▲▲▲

I love Haitian food. I visited Haiti in 2011. While I was there, I ate Lambi Boukannen (Grilled Conch). It was delightful.

Liliane Nerette-Louis, Storyteller

▲▲▲▲▲▲▲▲▲▲▲▲▲▲▲▲▲▲▲▲▲▲▲▲▲

My favorite Haitian food is Soup Joumou (Pumpkin Soup). I recall as a child that while my parents and their friends were celebrating the New Year, drinking and dancing in the living room, at around 5:00 a.m., my grandmother would quietly go to the kitchen and begin the preparation for the Soup.

The process seemed almost like a ritual. I would watch as she gathered the ingredients, and have the pot on the stove to have it all meld together into that golden, almost precious elixir. By sunrise, the Soup was ready and the adults would make their way into the kitchen. As a child, I hated having Soup for breakfast, but I cherish it now. Soup Joumou truly represents Haiti, and our resiliency as a strong, courageous people.

Rodney Pepe-Souvenir, Lawyer

▲ ▲

I love to eat Fritay. Not only for their taste, but mostly for the memories they bring back. My family always shared the story of the time I was a toddler in Haiti. I used to stay in front of the house in my diapers, waiting for the Fritay vendor to pass by.

I also love Diri ak Sòs Pwa. I always say, "If there's no rice, there's no food." Rice is an important element in Haitian cuisine. As Haitians, we were introduced to it at an early age. It is what we eat the most.

Vladimir Lévêque, Sound Engineering Student

▲ ▲

The list of my favorite Haitian foods is quite long. Although I became a vegetarian at the age of 16, I essentially enjoy all of our staple dishes - as long as it doesn't have meat or fish. I love, of course, the very delicious Diri ak Djon-Djon, Diri ak Sòs Pwa, Makawoni au Graten (Macaroni and Cheese), Banan Peze, Salade Russe, Legim (Legumes), and who can forget Pikliz to top it all off.

I enjoy not only the delicious taste, the flavorful spices, and the savory aroma of the food, but also the memories of growing up in a Haitian family where these dishes were at the center of our celebrations and get-togethers.

My fondest memories are of the Thanksgiving dinners I attended every year at my aunt's home. There was always an elaborate spread including all the dishes I mentioned; and, plenty of laughter, hugs, and reminiscing. For those reasons, Haitian food is my comfort food and reminds me of so many wonderful memories from my childhood and adolescence.

Mathylde Frontus, Ph.D., Adjunct Assistant Professor
at Columbia University

▲ ▲

For me, it's always a pleasure to eat Haitian food at restaurants and friends' parties. When I'm at home, I love to prepare different kinds of dishes. I love seafood, chicken, the National Rice, plantains, and Pikliz, which is a very spicy cabbage salad.

I love to finish dinner with dessert such as sweet potato bread. It is deliciously good. I love to have this creamy beverage made with milk, coconut, sugar, vanilla, and vodka. It always makes me happy when I get friends together to eat, talk, and drink a glass of wine as we listen to music.

Guerda Noel, Entrepreneur

▲ ▲

I was raised in L'Artibonite, Haiti. My favorite Haitian foods are white rice, Lalo (Jute Leaves), Kalalou, and Sòs Pwa.

A well-cooked and delicious Lalo is something that I can never forget. When I visit family in New Jersey, I eat it. Certainly, there are other Haitian foods that I enjoy such as Legumes Militon (Chayote) and Legumes Beregene (Eggplant).

Serge Renaud,
Founding Member of the National Alliance for the Advancement of Haitian Professionals (NAAHP)

▲ ▲

My favorite thing about Haitian food is that the flavors in the food are absolutely unmatched. No other culture's food compares in flavor to that of Haiti's. I have been eating Haitian food for as long as I can remember; and, every time I do, it feels like I am taking a bite out of the country. I feel wholesome and complete when I eat Haitian food - there's just something about it. Every time I do anything Haitian-related - from listening to the music to wearing the traditional clothing - I get an amazing feeling. Indulging in the culture makes me feel complete!

Yvana Romelus, Radio Personality

▲ ▲

I love to eat Legim (Legumes). My grandmother used to make it when I would visit her. She used to make Chaka as well.

Suze Guillaume,
Mother, Entrepreneur, Author, and Changemaker

▲ ▲

I went on a summer vacation to Haiti in 2001, and toured some of the most beautiful parts of the country (i.e. Jacmel, Cap Haitien, Lazile, etc.). I got to experience the different regional dishes which were always made with love.

At a beach in Jacmel, I tasted Lambi Boukannen (Grilled Conch) for the first time. I tried to make this mouth-watering dish on a few occasions, but I could never get the right taste as the first time I tried it.

Myrlande Georges, Social Worker & Designer

▲▲▲▲▲▲▲▲▲▲▲▲▲▲▲▲▲▲▲▲▲▲▲▲▲▲

I was born in Haiti and migrated to Brooklyn, New York in the 1980s. I grew up in a traditional Haitian household. Having a home-cooked meal every night was normal! My mother was, and still is, a great cook. Every New Year's Day, her Soup Joumou was requested by many, even our non-Haitian friends.

My mother would make a certain dish for every special occasion or when I did something amazing at school like making Honor Roll. The dish was called Poul Nan Sos (Chicken in Sauce). I remember how it made me feel. It felt as though there were no worries in the world; and, the most important thing was my plate of food. Now that I'm an adult, I've asked my mom how to prepare Poul Nan Sos so I can cook it for myself. I have a one-year old son, and I would love for him to share some of those memories surrounding Haitian food and culture.

Dr. Jean Alerte,
Owner of the Brooklyn Swirl & ACA Branding Agency

▲▲▲▲▲▲▲▲▲▲▲▲▲▲▲▲▲▲▲▲▲▲▲▲▲▲

I do like Griot and Patés. I had some in Haiti during my first visit there and they were amazing. I especially loved the pickled hot peppers that came with the Griot!

Abigail Lowe, Educator

▲ ▲

My favorite Haitian foods are Diri Djon-Djon, Makawoni au Graten, and Stewed Lambi. I remember my first trip to Haiti in 2014. In the morning, I ate fried breadfruit for the first time. At night, I had fresh lobsters over an open flame in Saint-Louis-du-Sud. The only light came from a generator.

Richard Louissaint, Photographer

▲ ▲

I love Diri Blan, Sos Pwa Blan, and Poul Nan Sos. My mom would cook big meals on Sunday mornings after Mass. I can remember standing next to her as she cooked. She would ask me to taste the food and tell her what's missing, "Sal manke?" (Is it missing salt?); or, if it's tasteful! By dinnertime, I was practically full because I helped taste the food entire time!

Another favorite dish of mine is Fritay. As a child, my parents made it very clear that, although I was born in Brooklyn, I was Haitian, not American. This meant I traveled to Haiti every year and spoke only Creole at home. I can remember walking around Port-Au-Prince with my dad. He once purchased a plate of Fritay, which included Banan Peze, Pikliz, Tassot, and even Pate Kode (Fried Patties). I was hooked on Fritay from that moment on!

Tamarre Torchon,
Director at Solid Foundation Academy

▲▲▲▲▲▲▲▲▲▲▲▲▲▲▲▲▲▲▲▲▲▲▲▲

Haitian cuisine is so exquisite that I love most of our meals but some more than others. My favorite Haitian dish is Conch (Lambi). I love it grilled with lime and lots of Pikliz and hot sauce. The fishermen at the beach make it best. Although most people will favor Griot, and Rice and Beans, I would choose Mayi Moulen, Diri Djon-Djon, or Sòs Pwa. Tchaka Mayi is another favorite along with Pintade (Guinea Fowl) and goat. I like the latter very well-spiced and grilled.

I must not forget the traditional Soup Joumou on January 1st. We have it in Haiti every Sunday. I don't consume it as much as I would like in the US, but it's a must have once in Haiti.

My list could go on and on. I would like to mention Bouyon ak Doumbrey (Soup with Dumplings), Akra, Banan Peze, and Makawoni au Graten. Salade Russe (Beet and Potato Salad) is my favorite kind of salad.

I love to be in Haiti around Easter. As a Catholic, I don't eat meat during Lent. After church on Good Friday, I always look forward to a great meal afterwards. Pwason Salé (Salted Fish), where it has been drying in the sun for weeks, will be served. It is cooked with lots of shallots. This is the only time of the year that I eat this type of fish. It is usually served with a good Salad Russe, and white rice with Sòs Pwa Blan (White Bean Sauce).

Nadine St. Julien, Traveler

117

▲▲▲▲▲▲▲▲▲▲▲▲▲▲▲▲▲▲▲▲▲▲▲▲▲▲▲

I would have to say hands down my favorite Haitian food would have to be Patés - whether it's filled with chicken or herring. Patés was a treat for me as a child like candy. It wasn't given to me often, but whenever I had it, I savored the moment.

My mother and I used to go to this Haitian Bakery called Le Foyer. Le Foyer was, and still, is the spot for Haitian baked snacks located in the busy city of Mattapan, Massachusetts known for welcoming multiple generations of Haitian immigrants.

When eating Patés, I had a method. I would peel off the flaky outer crusts like slices, and remove the beef. Once the outer layers were eaten, I'd carefully open the beef pouch and scrape out the beef, leaving a few bits of beef and seasoning inside the pouch. I'd then eat the smooth intact pouch. Lastly, the beef was left, and I'd devour that, too. Patés is as memorable to my childhood as popsicles in the summers.

Vie Ciné, Author

▲ ▲

Other than eating at home that always brings a kind of comfort comparable to nothing else, the most memorable time I have of eating Haitian food is when I eat the meals outside of Port-au-Prince. Seafood by the sea is always an unforgettable experience, especially because it's so fresh.

Keylah Mellon, Photographer

▲ ▲

I love Tassot and Fried Red Snapper with Banan Peze. I cook them at home, including baked turkey with red or black beans and white rice.

Cathy Delaleu, Writer, Poet, and Artist

▲ ▲

My favorite Haitian dish is Legim (Legumes). Growing up, my grandmother made the best Legim. It was the only way I would eat vegetables. It is actually the only Haitian dish I can make. The first time I attempted to make it on my own, I had both my sisters on a conference call and my mom on Skype. It turned out ok. It does take a lot of practice. Not everyone can make good Legim.

Vicki Sylvain, Founder of The Shoe-B

▲▲▲▲▲▲▲▲▲▲▲▲▲▲▲▲▲▲▲▲▲▲▲▲▲▲▲

I love almost all Haitian dishes, but some of my favorites are Diri Djon-Djon, Lambi, Sos Pwa, and Legim (Legumes).

I have women in my family that can really cook amazing Haitian food. When my mother cooks on special holidays, for some reason, the food just tastes so much more delicious than on regular days. I always look forward to dinner invites from my beloved cousin, Marie Pierre. She has mastered the art of traditional Haitian cuisine.

Jasmine Belotte, Co-Founder, Poised With Purpose

▲▲▲▲▲▲▲▲▲▲▲▲▲▲▲▲▲▲▲▲▲▲▲▲▲▲

The cuisine of a nation is an integral component of its folklore and cultural heritage. I am reminded of the healthy consumption patterns from my childhood and adolescent years - long before the Haitian agriculture and production were undermined by the United States with the complicity of the Haitian government, as well as the excessive liberalization of the Haitian economy. Until the year 1985, as far I recall, Haitian people, generally used to consume foods produced mainly in Haiti.

As far I am concerned, my favorite dishes are intimately related to my childhood in my hometown of Torbeck, in the South Department of Haiti. I remember that the foods were fresh, natural, and succulent, and prepared by my mother, Rose Marie aka Dedette. My dad also cooked for us. Most of these foods were grown either in my father's gardens or bought in the local market of Labathe, Gauvin, Labeï, Chantal, or Ducis.

My favorites are Tomtom with okra sauce and crawfish and Potage with Mazombèl. I truly enjoyed eating potatoes boiled in cow's milk. My father owned a herd of cows. My absolute favorite was the food served at home on Sundays. Generally, my mother prepared and served Diri National (using the real Madame Gougouse) accompanied by vegetables, meats, and bean sauce.

Jean Eddy Saint Paul, PhD.,
Sociologist, Founding Director of the City University of
New York's Haitian Studies Institute, and Professor of
Haitian Heritage at Brooklyn College

123

▲ ▲

I have the following fond memories of eating Haitian food:

As a kid, bonding with my paternal grandma while eating grilled peanuts on the steps of our house.

Eating Fritay with my friends at night. Banan Peze must be one of the best things on earth!

Seafood that's fresh from the sea and grilled right in front of you on the beach.

Celebrating finals with different kinds of Kleren or Tafia such as Sele Bride, Kremas, Prestige etc.

I almost forgot Soup Joumou, which became even more significant after I moved to the U.S.A.

Alexandra Spesest, Accountant and Social Entrepreneur

124

▲ ▲

My favorite Haitian dish is actually Squash Soup. In my family, the only time we make soup is on Haitian Independence Day. My children look forward to it every year. Even though I make my own soup, my mother always sends me a plate of her own. My husband is always in charge of getting the freshest Haitian bread for the soup. My kids help around with peeling the potatoes, radishes, and sometimes, Malanga (Taro Root).

On January 1st, which is Haitian Independence Day, we do not cook any other food. We eat soup all day. It's also around this meal that my brothers and sisters and their kids gather together to sit and talk about old times. We always end up reminiscing about our time growing up in the countryside of Haiti. It's a great family tradition.

Some of my children's friends are not Haitian. When they visit us on that day, they're always interested in learning about our culture and the history of our Squash Soup, and then they grab a plate and share in our tradition. I am thankful for the privilege of living in the USA, a land of many opportunities and great people, and I am honored to keep this Haitian tradition alive in my family.

Mandaly C. Louis-Charles,
Founder of www.sweetcoconuts.blogspot.com
and www.Creolelingo.com

▲ ▲

I love Haitian food, particularly Makawoni au Graten, Bouyon, and Tomtom ak Kalalou.

Steve Similien, Medical Professional

▲▲▲▲▲▲▲▲▲▲▲▲▲▲▲▲▲▲▲▲▲▲▲▲

My favorite Haitian foods are Akra, Bouyon, Soup Joumou, and Tassot Cabrit. The one thing I do not like is Sòs Pwa. When I was a kid, my great-grandmother, MaChimene, would greet me at the kitchen table with a bowl of Sòs Pwa with Banan. I'd have to sit there and eat the whole bowl before I could play. It would take me forever. I always appreciated her cooking for me though. I could always feel her love. She passed away almost two years ago; and, food is one of the ways I stay connected to her. It's how I remember her.

Jasmyn Crawford,
Marketing & Events Coordinator, Grandchamps

▲▲▲▲▲▲▲▲▲▲▲▲▲▲▲▲▲▲▲▲▲▲▲▲

Mwen renmen Banan Dous ak Labouyi.
(I love Sweet Plantains and Flour Porridge.)

Grandma Philomène Beaubrun

Let's Eat Haitian Food

Recipes

There's nothing else in this world quite like Haitian food – *Manje Ayisyen*. Haitian cuisine reflects the country's rich cultural heritage with French, African, Taino, and Spanish influences. It is unique in the use of herbs and spices, preparations and techniques, and rich and aromatic flavors.

I am sure you worked up an appetite for Haitian cuisine by now. In this section, I include recipes for some of my favorite Haitian foods. For me, learning how to cook Haitian food was a visceral learning experience. It was empowering to know that I was eating the same food my ancestors probably consumed for generations.

I sought advice from relatives and friends, and engaged in conversations with chefs and restaurant owners to perfect the recipes. I loved using the *pilón* (wooden mortar and pestle) to crush the garlic and onions. I also discovered that the pungent smell that always seemed to linger on my clothes and hair was actually from the *Jirof* (cloves) used to season meat, soups, etc. I'm not too fond of cloves, and I have eliminated them from my recipes.

I once met a restaurant owner at a community event in celebration of Haitian Heritage Month in Brooklyn, NY. We had an extensive discussion on the best way to cook *Banan Peze* to obtain that crunchy goodness. I also met another owner of a Haitian restaurant located in Fort Greene, Brooklyn. During our conversation, he stressed the importance of maximizing the use of every ingredient in every recipe.

In a Haitian kitchen, we don't necessarily use measuring cups or spoons. We have the uncanny ability to add just the right amount of seasoning, spice, or salt. However, this process won't necessarily work for those

130

who are new to Haitian cuisine. I had to make observations in the kitchens of relatives, and try out the recipes myself.

During the five years of my cultural journey, I amassed over 100 recipes of the meals I had eaten as a child. (I only included eleven of my most favorite recipes in this section.) These several recipes provide an overview of Haitian cuisine. The classics like *Banan Peze*, *Griot*, and *Diri Djon-Djon* are included. (Just a note: For more recipes, please check out my "Cook Like a Haitian" cookbook series on Amazon.com).

Every household has its own variation of a recipe. For example, in making *Diri Djon-Djon*, some would use butter while others would use olive oil, vegetable oil, or corn oil. These differences are not major, but the essence of the dish remains the same.

Haitian cooking is truly an act of love. You must be present in the moment. If your mind is elsewhere, the food won't come out tasty. As you make each meal, put your heart, mind, and soul into it. I guarantee you that it will make a huge difference. This is the ultimate reason why my Haitian brothers and sisters and I felt a great connection to Haiti through its food. We tasted the love that was put into it. Those who cooked our meals knew that they were not only nourishing our bodies but also our souls.

Bon Apeti,

Cindy Similien-Johnson

Banan Peze
(Fried Plantains)

One of the first things I learned how to cook was Banan Peze. Fried green plantains are a staple in every Haitian meal, and are usually served with fried meat such as Griot (fried pork).

INGREDIENTS
2 green plantains
2 cups olive oil
1 teaspoon salt
½ cup of water
1 juiced lime
1 tablespoon white vinegar

PREPARATION
1. Cut off ends of plantains. Peel and remove skins. Cut plantains into 1 ½ inch-thick diagonal pieces

2. Heat oil in a pan over medium heat for about one minute. Cook plantains three minutes on each side, or until they are light brown.

3. Remove plantains from heat. Using a Tostonera, or the bottom of a small plate, lightly flatten the plantains. Set aside.

4. In a small bowl, mix water, salt, lime juice, and white vinegar. Dip each plantain in water mixture, and cook the

plantains in pan for one minute on each side, or until golden brown and crispy. (Be careful. Hot oil will spatter!)

5. Remove plantains from pan, and place them on paper towels to remove excess oil.

Marinad ak Mori
(Codfish Fritters)

On Saturday mornings, I would eat Marinad ak Mori for breakfast alongside scrambled eggs. These codfish fritters are crunchy with a savory taste.

INGREDIENTS
½ pound codfish
2 eggs
2 garlic cloves, minced
1 onion, finely chopped
2 scallion stalks, chopped
½ teaspoon thyme
½ teaspoon parsley
1 teaspoon baking powder
2 cups all-purpose flour
a pinch of sugar
a pinch of black pepper
½ cup water
½ teaspoon hot pepper sauce
2 cups olive oil

PREPARATION
1. Soak codfish in water for at least 5 hours, or overnight. Or, rinse with water several times to decrease saltiness.

2. Bring 3 cups of water to a boil, and add codfish. Cook for 30 minutes, or until tender. Remove and shred codfish. Let cool for 10 minutes.

3. In a mixing bowl, combine codfish with the rest of the ingredients except the oil. Set aside.

4. Heat oil in a large pan over medium heat. Pour batter by spoonfuls into the hot oil. Cook at least 5 at a time for 2 minutes on each side, or until golden brown.

5. Remove the fritters from the pan, and blot on paper towel to remove excess oil.

Griot
(Fried Pork)

This is one of the most popular Haitian dishes. Marinated chunks of pork is broiled and then fried for that crispy brown glaze. This dish is served at all kinds of celebrations, including birthdays, weddings, graduations, baptisms, communions, etc. A Haitian party isn't a party without Griot!

INGREDIENTS
3 lbs pork shoulder, cubed
1 sour orange, juiced (keep grinds)
½ cup lime juice
2 bouillon cubes
3 garlic cloves. chopped
2 teaspoons parsley
1 onion, chopped
1 medium green pepper, chopped
1 teaspoon salt
1 teaspoon black pepper
2 cups olive oil

PREPARATION
1. In a bowl, mix salt, sour orange juice, and lime juice. Soak meat in mixture for 5 minutes. Rub meat with sour orange grinds, and rinse with water. Set meat aside.

2. In a bowl, combine crushed bouillon cubes, garlic, parsley, onions, salt, green pepper, and black pepper. Add

meat, and mix thoroughly. Let it marinate in refrigerator for 30 minutes, or overnight.

3. Place meat and marinade in a pot. Add just enough water to cover meat. Cook meat for 15 minutes or until meat is tender. Drain meat, and set aside.

4. Heat oil in pan over medium-high heat. Cook meat for 10 minutes, or until dark brown. Remove meat from pan, and place them on paper towels to remove excess oil.

Pikliz
(Coleslaw)

This spicy coleslaw is made with cabbage and other vegetables. It's usually served with Banan Peze and Griot.

INGREDIENTS
2 cups cabbage, thinly sliced
2 carrots, shredded
4 Scotch Bonnet Peppers, thinly sliced and stems removed
1 medium onion, thinly sliced
¼ teaspoon black pepper
1 teaspoon salt
4 garlic cloves, whole
½ cup lime juice
1 medium red bell pepper, thinly sliced
1 medium green bell pepper, thinly sliced
1 medium yellow bell pepper, thinly sliced
White vinegar
Glass jar with lid

PREPARATION
1. In a mixing bowl, combine all ingredients (except vinegar). Then, stuff mixture into glass jar. Add enough vinegar to cover the ingredients in the jar. Tightly cover jar, and marinate in refrigerator for 3-4 days before serving. It can last for two weeks.

Salad Jardiniere
(Haitian Salad)

This salad is so simple to make - just gather a colorful array of mixed vegetables, put them together, and you have a healthy salad, with a Haitian flair!

INGREDIENTS
1 head iceberg lettuce (rinsed, dried, and shredded)
1 medium red onion, sliced
1 medium green pepper, sliced
1 medium red pepper, sliced
1 cucumber, peeled and sliced
3 carrots, shredded
3 tomatoes, sliced
1 tablespoon olive oil
a dash of black pepper

PREPARATION
1. Combine all ingredients in a large bowl.

2. Serve plain, or with your favorite dressing.

Salade Russe
(Potato & Beet Salad)

The unique red color of this creamy potato salad comes from the juices of the beets.

INGREDIENTS
6 medium-sized potatoes, peeled
3 carrots, peeled
2 large beets
1 tablespoon minced onions
3 tablespoons mayonnaise
1 tablespoon melted butter
½ tablespoon fresh parsley, chopped
½ teaspoon black pepper
salt

PREPARATION
1. In one pot, bring to boil 4 cups of water, and add ½ teaspoon of salt. Add beets and boil for 30 minutes over medium-high heat, or until tender.

2. In the meantime, bring 4 cups of water to boil in another pot, add ½ teaspoon of salt. Boil potatoes and carrots together for 30 minutes over medium high heat.

3. Drain the beets, potatoes, and carrots and let them cool for 15 minutes in the refrigerator. Dice the potatoes and chop the carrots. Peel and dice the beets.

4. In a small bowl, stir mayonnaise, butter, parsley, black pepper, and ¼ teaspoon salt until mixed well.

5. Add the potatoes, carrots, and beets to the mayonnaise mixture. Mix well. Serve hot or cold.

Diri Djon-Djon
(Black Mushroom Rice)

This is a native dish of Haiti. The edible black mushrooms (Djon-Djon) give this rice dish its unique grayish-black coloring and distinctive flavor.

INGREDIENTS
2 cups dried Black Mushrooms (Djon-Djon)
4 cups jasmine rice, washed
1 cup pigeon peas, cooked
1 medium green pepper, chopped
2 garlic cloves, minced
1 small onion, minced
1 scallion stalk, chopped
4 fresh rosemary sprigs
1 whole Scotch Bonnet Pepper
1 tablespoon olive oil
2 tablespoons butter
2 chicken bouillon cubes
1 teaspoon salt

PREPARATION
1. In a medium pot, soak the Djon-Djon in 6 cups of water for 10 minutes, and then boil in the same water for 10 minutes over medium-high heat. Strain mushrooms, and reserve 4 cups of the black stock. Set aside.

2. In a medium pot, heat oil over medium heat. Sauté green pepper, garlic, onions, and scallions for 4-5 minutes. Add

pigeon peas. Stir for one minute. Add 4 cups of the black stock, and bring to a boil.

3. Add butter, crushed bouillon cubes, and salt. Stir in rice. Top with Scotch Bonnet Pepper. Reduce heat, cover pot, and cook for 20-25 minutes.

4. Remove pot from stove. Remove Scotch Bonnet Pepper. Fluff rice with fork.

Soup Joumou
(Pumpkin Soup)

This savory soup is served every New Year to celebrate Independence Day when Haiti became the first Black Republic on January 1, 1804. Pumpkin soup is also served on Thanksgiving and Christmas.

INGREDIENTS

For Meat:
1 lb beef chuck, cut in ½-inch pieces
1 lime, juiced (keep rinds)
1 large onion, diced
¼ teaspoon thyme
3 sprigs of parsley
¼ teaspoon black pepper
2 teaspoons salt
2 chicken bouillon cubes
2 tablespoons tomato paste
1 tablespoon olive oil

For Soup:
2 lbs pumpkin, diced in big chunks
5 medium potatoes, cubed
3 cups shredded cabbage
4 carrots, peeled and sliced
2 scallions, sliced
2 celery stalks, cut in ½-inch pieces
1 Scotch Bonnet Pepper, whole
½ cup vermicelli

INGREDIENTS (continued)
For Dumplings:
2 cups all-purpose flour
½ cup water
¼ teaspoon salt
¼ teaspoon black pepper
½ tablespoon oil

PREPARATION
1. In a medium bowl, add lime juice and meat. Rub meat with rinds. Rinse meat with lukewarm water. Set meat aside. Add onion, thyme, parsley, black pepper, salt, chicken bouillon cubes, and tomato paste to meat. Rub the seasoning into the meat. Let marinate in refrigerator for 30 minutes, or overnight.

2. In the meantime, puree pumpkin with 1 cup of water (or as much needed) in a blender. Set aside.

3. In a large pot, heat oil over medium heat. Add meat (without the marinade). Brown meat for 10 minutes, and remove from pot. Add 6 cups of water to the pot, and bring it to a boil. Stir in meat, pumpkin puree, marinade, potatoes, cabbage, carrots, and celery. Top with whole Scotch Bonnet Pepper (including the stem). Bring to a boil again.

4. Cover pot, lower heat to a simmer, and cook for 30 minutes. (Stir occasionally to make sure bottom doesn't get burned.)

5. Remove the Scotch bonnet Pepper. (Do not let it burst. If it does, your soup will be very spicy!) Add the vermicelli. Cook for another 10 minutes.

6. Dumplings: In a bowl, mix flour, water, salt, black pepper, and oil. Take 1 tablespoon of dough, and with the palm of your hands, roll dough into elongated shapes. Add dumplings to soup. Cook for 15 minutes. (Add more water to make soup less thick, if necessary.) Remove pot from heat.

Akasan
(Cornmeal Drink)

This popular Haitian beverage is very smooth and creamy. It's known for its rich sweetness, and it can be served hot or cold.

INGREDIENTS

2 cinnamon sticks
5 anise stars
1 cup very fine corn flour
1 teaspoon vanilla extract
1 cup cold milk

1 can evaporated milk
½ cup brown sugar
¼ teaspoon salt
lemon zest

PREPARATION

1. In a bowl, mix corn flour and cold milk until there are no lumps. Set aside.

2. In a pot, bring 4 cups of water to a boil. Add salt, cinnamon sticks, and anise stars. Boil for another 10 minutes. Lower the heat, and slowly pour the corn flour mixture into the boiling water. Keep stirring until liquid thickens.

3. Stir in sugar and vanilla extract. Slowly pour the evaporated milk into mixture, stirring constantly. Add lemon zest, and stir mixture. Cook for five minutes.

4. Remove from heat. Let mixture cool for 10 minutes. Remove anise and cinnamon sticks before serving in a bowl or cup.

Konparèt
(The Bread of Jeremie)

Konparèt is known as the bread of Jeremie, a province in Haiti known as the city of poets. Made with fresh coconut, ginger, and cinnamon, this bread-like cake with a thick crust has a sweet aroma.

INGREDIENTS
2 ½ cups all-purpose flour
1 tablespoon ground cinnamon
¼ teaspoon salt
1 teaspoon baking powder
2 eggs
4 tablespoons butter
½ cup brown sugar
½ cup honey
2 tablespoons fresh ginger, peeled and grated
½ teaspoon pure almond extract
1 teaspoon pure vanilla extract
2 teaspoons lime zest
1 ½ cup coconut flakes (or fresh grated coconut)

PREPARATION
1. Preheat oven to 350° F. Generously grease a sheet pan (with butter or non-stick cooking spray).

2. In a medium bowl, mix flour, cinnamon, salt, and baking powder. Set aside.

3. In another medium bowl, combine eggs, butter, sugar, and honey. Add ginger, almond extract, vanilla extract, lime zest, and coconut. Mix well.

4. Slowly add flour mixture to egg mixture. Mix until dough is formed. Mold dough into a ball. Transfer the ball onto greased sheet pan.

5. Bake for 30 minutes, or until golden brown. Let cool for 30 minutes before serving.

Peanut Candy
(Tablèt Pistache)

These candies are delightful treats made with peanuts. In Haiti, you will always see these delectable candies sold on every street corner.

INGREDIENTS
1 ½ cup brown sugar
1 cup salted peanuts
2 teaspoons ground ginger
2 teaspoons ground cinnamon
1 teaspoon pure vanilla extract
Pinch of salt
½ cup water

PREPARATION
1. Combine sugar and ½ cup of water in a medium saucepan. Cook for 3 minutes, or until sugar begins to dissolve.

2. Add peanuts, ginger, cinnamon, vanilla extract, and salt. Continue to cook for 10-15 minutes over medium-high heat, or until mixture thickens and turns golden amber. Stir occasionally. (Don't let pan burn.)

3. Remove pan from heat. Quickly pour and spread peanut mixture onto greased pan using a greased metal spatula. Let it cool completely for about 15 minutes. Break into even pieces.

A Glimpse of Haiti

History, Language, Literature, Music, and Culture

Flag of Haiti

Haitian Flag Description: The flag of Haiti consists of two equal sized horizontal stripes - the top one is blue and the bottom one is red. In the center of the Haitian flag is the country's coat of arms, placed on a white square. The coat of arms consists of a Palmette surrounded by the liberty cap, and under the palms a trophy with the inscription: "L'Union Fait la Force," which means "In Union There Is Strength."

Haitian Flag Meaning: The Haitian flag is an adaptation of the French national flag. The blue stripe represents the union of black Haitians and mulatto Haitians, who are represented by the red stripe.

Haitian Flag History: The current Haitian flag was adopted on February 26, 1986. Haiti declared independence from France on January 1, 1804. The Haitian flag was originally blue and red vertical stripes, which was an adaptation of the French national flag. The white stripe of the French flag was omitted because it represented white colonial oppression. The vertical stripes were changed to horizontal stripes in the mid-19th century.

Sources: www.ijdh.org and worldflags101.com

Map of Haiti

Haiti is a country in the Caribbean Sea that occupies the western third of the island of Hispaniola. It is bordered by the Dominican Republic in the east.

With an area of 27,750 km², the country is slightly smaller than Albania, or slightly smaller than the U.S. state of Maryland. It is the most mountainous country in the Caribbean, its highest point is Pic la Selle (Chaine de la Selle) with 2,680 m (8,793 ft). Haiti has a population of 10 million people. Its capital is Port-Au-Prince.

Source: nationsonline.org

Facts About Haiti

1. Haiti's motto is: "L'Union Fait La Force" (Union Makes Strength).

2. Its official languages are French and Creole.

3. Haiti is the most mountainous nation in the Caribbean. The country's name came from an Arawak Indian word meaning "land of mountains."

4. Haitian revolutionary leader Francois-Dominique Toussaint earned the nickname Toussaint-L' Ouverture (the opening), which referred to his ability to find an opening in the enemy lines as well as opening the way for Haiti's independence.

5. Haiti is the first Black Republic in the world. It is the first country in the Western Hemisphere to abolish slavery. It is the second country in the world to issue a Declaration of Independence, only 33 years after the United States of America.

6. Haiti's national sport is soccer. Haiti first competed in the World Cup in 1974.

7. Haiti is the third largest country in the Caribbean, after the Dominican Republic and Cuba (which is the largest).

8. The capital Port-Au-Prince was founded in 1749 and was named for the Prince, a French ship anchored in the bay.

9. For much of the 17th and the 18th century, Haiti was responsible for 60% of the world's coffee exports.

10. Haitian currency is named after the gourd, a plant of the Cucurbitaceous family. Gourd is occasionally used to describe crops like pumpkins, cucumbers, squash and melons. Gourds were so important to the Haitian people that in 1807, President Henri Christophe (1761-1820) made them the base of national currency and declared all gourds the property of the state. Today, the Haitian currency is called "gourdes."

SOURCES: www.worldatlas.com & www.embassyofhaiti-rsa.org

A Short History About Haiti

In 1492, Christopher Columbus landed on the Caribbean island we now know as Haiti, claiming it for the Spanish, and naming it Hispaniola. Soon after this, the New World's first settlement was built at La Navidad on Haiti's north coast. The island remained under Spanish control until 1698, when, subsequent to the Treaty of Ryswick, it was split into two separate colonies; the Spanish stronghold of Santo Domingo, and France's colony, St. Domingue or "The Pearl of the Antilles," which would prove to be its most lucrative overseas territory.

The island was ruled over by these two colonial powers for the next 100 years, with trade in sugar, rum, coffee, and cotton flourishing. Meanwhile, the Spanish and French authorities were increasingly involved in the booming slave trade.

Jamaican-born Boukman was the first to sow the seeds of dissent by leading a slave revolt against the occupying powers in 1791. This broke out into a 13-year war of liberation waged by the slave armies on the colonists, and later Napoleon's army.

Toussaint L'Ouverture, the leader of the revolution, was deported to France by Napoleon Bonaparte in 1802, where he died a year later. His deputy General Jean-Jacques Dessalines took the reins and in 1803, the slave armies claimed victory over the French at the Battle of Vertières, and on January 1st of the following year Dessalines declared the second republic, and the island was re-named "Haiti," or "Ayiti" in Creole, meaning "mountainous country."

A mere two years after reclaiming its freedom from the French, Haiti returned to turmoil, with General Dessalines being assassinated in 1806, and a civil-war ravaging the country between 1807 and 1820. The island was divided into the northern kingdom of Henri Christophe and the southern republic governed by Alexandre Pétion. The conflict came to an end when Christophe, faced with a mutiny by his own men, was driven to suicide. After Cristophe's death in 1820, Jean-Paul Boyer took on the role of president of the entire republic, leading the Haitians to independence from Spain in 1821.

In 1838, France recognized Haitian independence, but at a high price. Haiti was forced to take out crippling loans in order to pay the 150 million franc indemnity demanded by the French for this "privilege." In the meantime, the island continued to be shunned by other nations on account of its unruly reputation.

In 1915, U.S. Marines occupied Haiti, seizing control of its ports and custom houses. Despite organized resistance, they did not withdraw until 1934. In 1937, tragedy struck Haiti, when the Dominican President, Rafael Trujillo, gave the order for his soldiers to massacre thousands of Haitians residing near the border of the Dominican Republic.

A series of failed attempts at democracy, military-controlled elections lead to Dr. Francois Duvalier being named President in 1957. The regime, as reinforced by the President's henchmen the "Tonton Macoute," became infamous for its brutality. In 1964, the corrupt Duvalier, better known as "Papa Doc," changed the constitution to make himself "President-for-Life." Tens of thousands of Haitians were killed or exiled during his ruthless dictatorship. Subsequent to Duvalier's death in 1971, the reins of power were handed to his 19-year-old son, Jean Claude aka "Baby-Doc." He equaled if not surpassed his father in cruelty, killing and torturing thousands. By the year of his ascendance to presidency, Haiti had become the poorest country in the western-hemisphere, and remains so to this day.

By 1986, massive demonstrations against Jean Claude Duvalier's tyranny led the U.S. to intervene by arranging his exile to France. General Henri Namphy took his place as the head of a National Governing Council, and the following year a new constitution was ratified. However, in November 1987, the general elections were soon abandoned after dozens of people were shot at by militants and the Tonton Macoute.

In 1988, military-controlled elections were held, and Leslie Manigat became Haiti's President. His ousting by General Namphy four months later would be the first in a chain of political upheavals. In November 1988, General Prosper Avril seized power from Namphy, heading up a repressive regime with widespread censorship in place. However, by 1990 popular protests and pressure from the American Ambassador convinced Avril to resign, with democratic elections taking place in December. Father Jean-Bertrand Aristide was named President with 67.5% of the vote.

On returning from addressing the UN General Assembly in 1991, President Aristide faced a violent coup d'état staged by the military, and was ousted. In the aftermath of the coup, the Organization of American States (OAS) called for an embargo on the de facto regime in

Haiti, but this ultimately failed as goods continued to be smuggled through the Dominican Republic.

In July 1993, President Aristide and General Raoul Cédras signed the Governors Island Accord, calling for the retirement of Cédras, the return of the President, and the formation and training of a new civilian police force. General Cédras refused to step down as promised, and there was further unrest. The embargo on Haiti was reinforced by the UN, and human rights observers were brought in. The following year a naval blockade was backed by Argentine, Canadian, French, Dutch and U.S. warships.

In September 1994, U.S. President Clinton formed a multinational force with 20 other nations, which proceeded to land on the island after the coup leaders agree to leave the country. On October 15th, the exiled President Aristide and his Government return to Haiti. Former Prime Minister, René Préval, won the elections to become President in December 1995.

Charges of corruption and fraud sullied the municipal and legislative elections of 2000, leading to a boycott of the presidential elections later that year, which were won by Aristide. By 2004, Haiti's economy was struggling, while human rights abuses and political violence were rife. This backdrop paved the way for yet another upheaval, with a rebel movement seizing power and forcing Aristide into exile.

During this tumultuous time, Boniface Alexandre assumed the interim authority, before René Préval was re-elected as President in February 2006. The elections were once again marred by corruption and uncertainty, and the United Nations Stabilization Mission in Haiti remained in the country, having arrived there during the 2004 Haiti Rebellion.

The catastrophic Haiti earthquake of 2010 had devastating effects, leaving up to 217,300 people dead and 2.1 million homeless. Presidential elections planned for January 2010 were subsequently postponed, and in April 2011, President Michel Martelly won a landslide victory.

Source: www.havenpartnership.com

Haitian Phrases

Haitian Creole: Bonjou! / Bon Maten!
English: Good morning!

Haitian Creole: Bon apre-midi!
English: Good afternoon!

Haitian Creole: Bonswa!
English: Good evening!

Haitian Creole: N a wè pi ta.
English: See you later.

Haitian Creole: Pase yon bònn jounen. / Bònn jounen.
English: Have a nice day.

Haitian Creole: Kouman ou rele?
English: What is your name?

Haitian Creole: M rele (your name).
English: My name is (your name).

Haitian Creole: Kouman ou ye? / Sak pase?
English: How are you?

Haitian Creole: N'ap boule!
English: Doing good!

Haitian Creole: Anchante.
English: Pleased to meet you.

Haitian Proverbs

Haitian Creole: Sa ou fe, se li ou we.
English: What you do is what you see.

Haitian Creole: Bondye do ou, Fe pa ou, M a fe pa M.
English: God says, Do your part; and, I'll do mine.

Haitian Creole: Bondye Bon.
English: God is good.

Haitian Creole: Dye mon, gen mon.
English: Beyond the mountains, more mountains.

Haitian Creole: Piti piti, zwazo fè nich.
English: Little by little birds build their nests.

Haitian Creole: Anpil men chay pa lou.
English: Many hands make a load lighter.

Haitian Creole: Sa ou plante se li ou rekolte.
English: What you sow is what you will harvest.

Haitian Creole: Sak pa bon pou youn, pi bon pou yon lot.
English: One man's trash is another's treasure.

Haitian Creole: Piti, piti wazo fe nich li.
English: Little by little, the bird builds its nest.

Haitian Creole: Sel pa vante tèt li di li sale.
English: Salt doesn't boast that it is salty.

Literature

1. **"Love, Anger, Madness"** by Marie Vieux-Chauvet

2. **"General Sun, My Brother"** by Jacques Stephen Alexis

3. **"Memoir of an Amnesiac"** by Jan J. Dominique

4. **"Anthologie Secrete"** by Ida Faubert

5. **"Masters of the Dew"** by Jacques Roumain

6. **"The Farming of Bones"** by Edwidge Danticat

7. **"Silencing the Past: Power and the Production of History"** by Michel-Rolph Trouillot

8. **"Haiti: The Aftershocks of History"** by Laurent Dubois

9. **"So Spoke the Uncle (Ainsi Parla l'Oncle)"** by Jean Price-Mars

10. **"The Making of Haiti"** by Carolyn Fick

11. **"Tropics of Haiti: Race and the Literary History of the Haitian Revolution in the Atlantic World, 1789-1865"** by Dr. Marlene Daut

Music

Haitian music has French, African, and Spanish elements. The most popular style is Kompa. (Thank you to Frederik Hahn aka "DJ HAITIAN STAR" and DJ/Producer Sabine Blaizin (Oyasound) for helping me put this list together.)

1. **"La Dessalinienne (The Dessalines Song)"** - the National Anthem of Haiti

2. **"Ayite Se"** by Mikaben

3. **"A.K.I.K.O."** by Emeline Michele

4. **"Zouk La Se Sel Medikaman Nou Ni"** by Kassav

5. **"Lakay"** by Tabou Combo

6. **"Lakòl"** by Claude Marcelin

7. **"Manman"** by Manno Charlemagne

8. **"Tu Me Touches"** by T-Vice

9. **"Si Bondye"** by Ansy & Yole Derose

10. **"Encore"** by Herve Gilbert

11. **"Kem Pa Sote"** by Boukman Eksperyans

12. **"Haiti Cherie"** by Georges Moustaki

Recommendations

Below are a few recommendations or resources on Haitian cuisine, community, and culture.

LANGUAGE

"Haitian Creole Phrasebook: Essential Expressions for Communicating in Haiti" by Jowel C. Laguerre

"Pawol Lakay: Haitian-Creole Language and Culture for Beginner and Intermediate Learners (Creole Edition)" by Frenand Leger

"Haitian Creole Dictionary and Phrasebook: Haitian Creole-English, English-Haitian Creole (Hippocrene Dictionary & Phrasebook)" by Charmant Theodore

The Haitian Creole Language Institute of New York
www.haitiancreoleinstitute.com
Offers classes in Haitian Creole

Sweet Coconuts
www.sweetcoconuts.blogspot.com
A resource and learning site for those who are learning to speak Haitian Creole

CUISINE

"Cook Like A Haitian" Cookbook Series
by Cindy Similien-Johnson

"A Taste of Haiti" by Mirta Yurnet-Thomas

"Haiti Uncovered: A Regional Adventure Into the Art of Haitian Cuisine" by Nadege Fleurimond

RESTAURANTS (IN NYC)

Grandchamps
www.grandchamps.nyc
A local family kitchen bringing the community together through Haitian cuisine in the heart of Bed-Stuy, Brooklyn

Kombit Restaurant
www.kombitrestaurant.com
Offers a menu of authentic Haitian Cuisine, deliciously prepared with organic spices

La Caye
www.lacayebk.com
Brings authentic Haitian cuisine to the heart of Fort Greene, Brooklyn

NEWS OUTLETS

The Haitian Times
www.haitiantimes.com
An online-only news publication which is the most authoritative voice for the Haitian Diaspora

Le Nouvelliste
www.lenouvelliste.com
A French-language daily newspaper printed in Port-au-Prince, Haiti, and distributed throughout the country, particularly the capital and 18 of the country's major cities

Haiti Libre
www.haitilibre.com
Government, civil society, economy, health, violence, environment, education and sports news from Haiti

Radio Soliel
www.radiosoliel.com
A twenty-four-hour Haitian Radio Station that broadcasts to the tri state area of NY, NJ and CT

CULTURAL CENTERS

Haiti Cultural Exchange
www.haiticulturalx.org
A nonprofit organization established to develop, present and promote the cultural expressions of the Haitian people

CULTURE

L'Union Suite
www.lunionsuite.com
A Haitian-American lifestyle, tourism, culture, society, and entertainment blog site

Kreyolicious
kreyolicious.com
A premier lifestyle, culture, and entertainment blog and brand of the hip, young, trend-oriented, forward thinking Haitian-Americans

About the Author

Cindy Similien-Johnson is guided by the principle: "Live to love; work to improve the lives of others; and, create a legacy." Her life's work includes the love of writing, women empowerment, and Haitian culture. A graduate of Barnard College-Columbia University, she is a prolific author of several books, including "How to Stay Motivated: Inspiration and Advice for Everyday Living"; "Living Expectantly: 30 Days to Living an Abundant Life"; and, "Goal Chic: Changing the World, One Goal at a Time." She founded CSJ Media Publishing to inspire, encourage, and empower through the written word. She is also a columnist for the Haitian Times.

With several years of experience in the non-profit sector, she founded Goal Chic, an initiative whose mission is to educate, engage, and empower women and girls in her community to be successful in their careers & purpose, personal finances, health & wellness, and relationships. In 2016, she was nominated and invited as a changemaker at the inaugural United State of Women Summit convened by First Lady Michelle Obama and the White House. The Summit rallied thought leaders, activists, community leaders, and citizens together to celebrate their achievements and create an action plan.

To stay connected to her Haitian roots, she founded "Cook Like a Haitian," a company whose mission is to introduce Haiti's cuisine, community, and culture to the world. A portion of all sales is donated to organizations who improve the lives of people of Haitian descent. As a Board Member of the United Nations Association-Brooklyn Chapter, Ms. Similien-Johnson brings awareness to global issues such as climate change, gender inequality, and child hunger.

Ms. Similien-Johnson has received numerous recognition for her outstanding and tireless efforts in her work as a community organizer, author, and cultural ambassador. Awards include the Star Network's 40 Stars Under Forty; PowerUP! KREYOL Business Competition Winner; the Caribbean American Chamber of Commerce and Industry, Inc.'s Caribbean-American Heritage Celebration Economic Development Award; and, the Caribbean Life Impact Award. She has been featured in leading publications and stations such as the New York Times, Amsterdam News, The Haitian Times, Face2Face Africa, Dominican Today, Our Time Press, the Word Network, and the African Caribbean Radio and Television (ACRTv).

Made in the USA
Las Vegas, NV
27 November 2024

12784690R00095